Children
and the
Holy Spirit

How to set your child's heart on fire for God

MARK HARPER

Mark Harper Ministries
PO Box 425
Sauk Rapids, MN 56379

ISBN 1-928866-00-X

For Worldwide Distribution
Printed in the U.S.A

First Printing 1999

This book is available at Christian bookstores
and distributors worldwide or directly through
Mark Harper Ministries.

Reach us on the Internet www.superchurch.com

Acknowledgements

First of all I want to say thank you to the servants of God who are leading this current revival from the many streams in the body of Christ. Thank you Rodney Howard-Brown, Kenneth Hagin, Randy Clark, John Arnott, John Kilpatrick and Steve Hill. Thank you for your obedience.

I would like to express my gratitude to several friends who have helped to make this book possible:

- To my wife Debra who has believed in me in the good times and the bad. Thank you also for word processing, editing and help with writing.
- To Leanna Willis for her help with writing and editing, especially when the heat is on.
- To Dave Carrick of Carrick Design, Inc. for always making us look good in print.
- To Gloria (Chick) Hardy and Mary Anderson for their excellent proofing and editing skills.
- To Erin Skillingstad for her ability to decipher my handwriting and type the original manuscript.
- To John Tasch, David Walters, and Vann Lane for your vision and for joining with me to **Lead The Children Into Revival!**

Mark Harper
Mark Harper Ministries
March 1999

CONTENTS

INTRODUCTION

Why Revival?

In Matthew 25, Jesus told a parable about ten virgins who took their lamps and went out to meet the bridegroom. Five were ready for the bridegroom's arrival, five were not. The ten virgins represent the Church, while the bridegroom represents the Lord Jesus Christ. Jesus was warning us to keep ourselves ready for His return.

To bring this parable closer to home, let's pretend you know a young lady named Sue who is about to get married to a young man named John.

You ask her, "Are you excited about getting married?"

She responds, "Oh, no big deal. I could take him or leave him."

What would you think? You'd probably think this girl is not ready to get married.

Folks, Jesus is coming back for a Church that is red hot and passionately in love with Him. And that is what revival does in the hearts of God's people: it stirs up our love for Jesus until nothing else matters but Him.

In the September 1998 issue of *Charisma* magazine, J. Lee Grady wrote, "I appreciate all the wonderful parenting advice that is available in Christian bookstores today. But, did you know that those books on discipline won't set your kid's heart on fire for God? Only the anointing of the Holy Spirit will produce children who have the same holy spunk that Jesus, Daniel, David, Esther, and Samuel had when they were youngsters."

That is what this book is all about: setting your child's heart on fire for God. I don't pretend to have all the answers, but I promise if you follow these steps with a sincere desire that you will see a change in your child's relationship with God.

CHAPTER ONE

"All Flesh"

In the summer of 1996, I was a senior pastor at a small church in Ontario, Canada, but I would minister at kids' camps from time to time. In August, I was ministering at a kids' camp in Minnesota. I was sitting behind the puppet stage, waiting to be introduced after praise and worship. The worship team, which was primarily teenagers, was singing the song, "Shout to the Lord."

I sensed the presence of God in a powerful way, even though I couldn't see anyone. I peeked my head out from behind the stage and saw an awesome sight. Every single child, all 75 of them, and all the counselors had their arms lifted up and were loving Jesus. Tears began to stream down my face as I watched these children. I had never seen children worship like this.

Yet the Word of God makes it clear that the Holy Spirit desires to move among the children:

> *And it shall come to pass in the last days, saith God, I will pour out of my Spirit upon all flesh: and your sons and your daughters shall prophesy, and your young men shall see visions, and your old men shall dream dreams...*
> *—Acts 2:17*

Unfortunately, we sometimes become so familiar with scriptures that we read them religiously and we miss what they are saying. Many people read this scripture like this: "He will pour out His Spirit upon all adults." At many of our Pentecostal churches, Mom and Dad are in the sanctuary having a Holy Ghost time while the kids are in the basement trying to figure out how many things you can make out of an egg carton. God said He would pour out His Spirit on all flesh, and that includes our youth and our children.

This error has been in the church since the days of the apostles. I think, basically, that the disciples were good men. They left everything to follow Jesus, but they were human just like the rest of us, and they had a wrong attitude about children.

MARK 10:13-15

13 And they brought young children to him, that he should touch them: and his disciples rebuked those that brought them.

14 But when Jesus saw it, he was much displeased, and said unto them, Suffer the little children to come unto me, and forbid them not: for of such is the kingdom of God.

15 Verily I say unto you, Whosoever shall not receive the kingdom of God as a little child, he shall not enter therein.

Listen to what Charles Hadden Spurgeon had to say about this verse:

Say not, the child may not come till he is a man, but know that you cannot come till you are like him. It is no difficulty in the child's way that he is not like you: the difficulty is with you, that you are not like the child. Instead of the child needing to wait until he grows up and becomes a man, it is the man who must grow down and become like a child.[1]

I ask you to take a moment to stop and check your heart. Mom and Dad, have you made the same mistake the disciples made? Have you pushed your children away from Jesus by having an attitude that revival is not for them? If so, just take a few moments to repent and ask Jesus to forgive you, and He will. Also, if you feel you should ask your children to forgive you, this will go a long way toward leading them into that passionate, love relationship with Jesus.

Pastor, Elder, Church Leader, have you had a wrong attitude about children and youth? Has your goal been to get them out of the service so you can have a "deeper move of God"? If so, ask Jesus to forgive and show you how to include children and youth in the move of God at your church.

IT STARTS WITH US

I was not always open to this move of God. Like many others, I had heard about the Holy Spirit being poured out in various places all around the world, but it seemed so strange. I wasn't sure it was really of the Lord.

That all changed for me in April of 1995. I had just assumed the pastorate of a struggling church in Sarnia, Ontario, Canada. I was living in a hotel room in Sarnia while my wife and two children were living in Brooklyn Park, Minnesota, until our house sold.

It was during this time that revival broke out in our home church, Living Word Christian Center, in Minneapolis. Debbie called me one day and said, "They had a four hour staff prayer meeting."

"Four hours!" I said.

I had spent sixteen years of my ministry ministering to children, and when you are a children's pastor, long services are not of God. At one camp meeting where I was ministering to 200 pre-school children, just the offering in the main service lasted 3 1/2 hours. That service lasted from 7:00 p.m. to 1:00 a.m. It didn't seem very spiritual from my perspective. I was worn out.

Debbie went on to explain that they were having nightly services at church and that wild and unusual manifestations were happening. I had heard about the laughter and Holy Ghost drunkenness, but like a lot of other people, I had dismissed it, saying, "It's not for me."

My first exposure to this type of manifestation was in 1985. I was children's pastor at Family Worship Center in Tulsa, Oklahoma. Dr. Ken Stewart was my pastor. Dr. Stewart was an awesome preacher, but there was very little move of the Spirit in church. One day Doc informed me that we were having a guest speaker by the name of Joe Jordan. The only thing Doc told me about Joe was that he had long services that sometimes lasted until midnight. (Again, not good news if you are the children's pastor.) I begged for mercy and we came to an agreement that I would minister to the children until 9:00 p.m., and at that time we would release the children into the adult service.

I was not prepared for what I saw that night. I had been saved and filled with the Holy Ghost since 1976, but I had never seen a service like that one. Joe prayed for our church secretary, Leona. Leona had a bad back. Joe had her sit down and stretch out her legs. One leg was longer than the other, so Joe prayed for her short leg to grow out. I had seen this many times, but what I had never seen before or since was when Joe stopped praying, Leona could not put her legs down—they were stuck in the air for 45 minutes.

There were many healings and unusual manifestations that night, but the most bizarre thing was what Joe called "being drunk in the Holy Ghost." The staff, my friends, and my pastor were rolling on the floor laughing hysterically and acting like drunk people. I did not understand what was going on, but I figured this out—if you got near one of the drunk people, you got it!

Now all of the children ran up to the front and followed Joe around, but I stood by the back wall singing, "I shall not be moved."

I had no idea what God was doing that night (except that many people did receive healings), but the next day Joe left town and everybody was back to normal. I didn't have to worry about it.

My next exposure was in July of 1993. I was speaking at a church near Ft. Worth, Texas. The pastor told me that there was an evangelist holding a revival meeting at Bob Nichol's church in Fort Worth. He invited me to go with him. We attended a morning meeting at a Rodney Howard Brown Crusade. The preaching was great. There was some laughter and drunkenness toward the end, but I just thought, "It's not for me."

What really got my attention, though, was when revival broke out at my home church, Living Word. Good friends of mine were changed overnight; they were totally different people. I attended a couple meetings at Living Word and I wanted to get prayed for, but I had too much pride. I didn't want to deal with the pressure of my friends expecting me to do something.

When I got back to my church in Canada, I heard about a revival that was happening at a church in Toronto, the Toronto Airport Vineyard Church. "This was perfect," I thought. "I'll go there and get prayed for. Nobody will know me in Toronto."

Debbie and I and our two children, Mark, Jr. and Melissa, loaded up in the car and headed for Toronto (about 2½ hours away.) The Toronto service was a mind-blower for me. We attended on a Tuesday night. There were about 1,500 people in attendance from 32 different nations and every denomination you can imagine: Baptist, Presbyterian, Anglican, Catholic, Assembly of God, Methodist, etc.

The leader of the meeting asked a Catholic priest to come up and testify. He testified about revival in his church. After testifying, they prayed for him, and he was "slain in the Spirit." Instead of lying on the ground, he bounced on the floor (about 16 inches off the ground) for several minutes. Then they asked all the Catholics to come forward to get prayed for. Most of them fell down and began to laugh, shake, and roll. In Toronto, I saw Catholics, Baptists, and Anglicans all get drunk in the Holy Ghost and manifest the Spirit in many different ways. I wanted to go to these people and say, " Hey, wait a minute, first you have to speak in tongues." I thought basic Pentecostal doctrine says first you speak in tongues, then you can do all that other stuff. These people were getting "filled with the Spirit" and they didn't talk in tongues yet.

I asked the Lord, "Is this right?"

The Holy Ghost spoke this scripture to my heart. "I will pour out my Spirit upon all flesh." I saw that night that God doesn't care as much as we do about our denominations or what kind of doctrine we have; the Holy Ghost responds to hungry hearts.

I was hungry. I laid down my preconceptions and my

pride… and jumped into the river of revival.

TAKE THIS REVIVAL TO THE CHILDREN

When I finally made the decision to jump into the river, the Spirit of God spoke to me, saying, "Take this revival to the children." I saw then that parents and church leaders have a major part to play in leading our children into a passionate love relationship with Jesus.

The devil is after our children. Kids face things in school today that we never had to face—things like drugs, guns, rape, and murder. Let's not deny our children the one thing they need to overcome temptation—the power of God. Children and youth today need the power of God; it's not an option.

We must do everything in our ability to make God's power available to them.

1 C. H. Spurgeon, *Come Ye Children,* (Pasadena, Texas: Pilgrim Publications), p. 50.

CHAPTER TWO

History Of Children In Revival

We will not keep them from our children; we will tell the next generation about the Lords' power and his great deeds and the wonderful things he has done... He instructed our ancestors to teach his laws to their children, so that the next generation might learn them and in turn should tell their children. In this way also they would put their trust in God and not forget what he has done, but always obey his commandments.

—Psalm 78:4-7 (GNB)

In chapter two, we will take a look at the history of children in revival. Whenever God was moving, children's lives were being changed. All throughout history. Yet today in America, when we mention the words "children's ministry," we think of Sunday school, Bible stories, flannel graphs, games, puppets, treats and crafts. It hasn't always been that way. One constant throughout history is that when God's Spirit is moving it has impacted children and teenagers in a powerful way.

Please don't misunderstand me. There are many valuable methods when teaching children, but they should not take precedent over the move of God's Spirit. Our number-one goal in children's ministry should be to cause children to have a passionate love relationship with Jesus.

As we take a look at the history of revival, we will see how many of the great revival leaders were impacted powerfully in their childhood or teenage years.

JONATHAN EDWARDS (1703-1758)

At age 17, after a period of distress, he said holiness was revealed to him as a ravishing, divine beauty. His heart panted "to lie low before God, as in the dust; that I might be nothing, and that God might be all, and that I might become as a little child." [1]

This doesn't sound like "teenage talk" to me. It sounds like the Spirit of God speaking. Jonathan Edwards went on to pastor at a North Hampton, Massachusetts, parish where revival broke out and spread to all of Connecticut. He was one of the leaders of the "Great Awakening" in North America. Some consider him to be the finest theologian America has produced.

GEORGE WHITEFIELD (1714-1770)

George Whitefield was born on December 16, 1714. In 1733, at the age of 18, while attending Oxford University, his life was changed forever.

...but Whitefield soon fell in with a group of pious

"Methodists" led by the Wesley brothers, John and Charles. Soon Whitefield was lost in the rigors of Methodist devotions that culminated in a highly personal and emotional "New Birth."

He determined to use the pulpit to bring others to a conversion experience. At Oxford it became clear to Whitefield he was no scholar, but equally clear he was a communicator without peer. With encouragement from the Wesley's, he determined to be a missionary to the new Georgia colony.

In the summer of 1736, while waiting to embark for Georgia, Whitefield was ordained a deacon in the Anglican church and began preaching in and around London. Wherever he spoke, crowds materialized and hung on every word of the "boy preacher's" dramatic delivery. [2]

Only the Spirit of God can cause this to happen, as many people would have too much pride to "hang on every word of a boy preacher."

Whitefield also seemed to have a powerful children's ministry as he records in a letter written in September of 1741.

On Monday morning, I visited the children in the three hospitals… On Thursday evening, I preached to the children of the city with a congregation of near 20,000 in the park. It is remarkable that many children are under convictions, and everywhere great power and apparent success attend the word preached. [3]

Wow! That's an awesome kid's crusade with 20,000 in attendance and no sound system, drama skits, or flannel graph stories. Only the power of God could cause this to happen.

In April of 1742, an Edinburgh minister wrote:

On June 3rd, Whitefield arrived for his second visit to a rapturous welcome, and the following morning, three of the little boys that were converted when I was last here, came to me and wept and begged me to pray for and with them. A minister tells me that scarce one is fallen back who was awakened, either among old or young. [3]

America's Great Awakening was sparked largely by Whitefield's preaching tour of 1739-40. Though only 25 years old, the evangelist took America by storm. Whitefield's farewell sermon on Boston Common drew 23,000 people—more than Boston's entire population. It was probably the largest crowd that had ever gathered in America. [4]

JOHN WESLEY (1703-1791)

It seems that John Wesley of the Methodist church and leader of the Wesleyan revival throughout England, also had a powerful ministry to children and was not too prideful to preach to children. The following are some quotes from John Wesley's journals.

April 11, 1756. (Dublin) I met about a hundred children, who are catechized (instructed) pubicly twice a week. Thomas Walsh began this some months ago, and the fruit of it appears already. What a pity, that all our Preachers in every place, have not the zeal and wisdom to follow his example.

July 30, 1758. (Cork) I began meeting with the children in the afternoon, though with little hopes of doing them good; but I had not spoken long on our natural state before many of them were in tears, and five or six so affected, that they could not refrain from crying aloud to God. When I began praying, their cries increased, so that my voice was soon lost. I have seen no such work among children for eighteen or nineteen years.

January 17, 1772. (Hertford) I found the poor children whom Mr. A kept at school were increased to about thirty boys and girls. I went in immediately to the girls. As soon as I began to speak, some of them burst into tears, and their emotion rose higher and higher. But it was kept within bounds until I began to pray.

A cry then arose, which spread from one to another, till almost all cried aloud for mercy, and would not be comforted. But how the scene was changed when I went to the boys! They seemed as dead as stones, and scarce appeared to mind anything that was said, nay, some of them could hardly refrain from laughter. However, I spoke on, and set before them the terrors of the Lord. Presently one was cut to the heart, soon after another, and another. In ten minutes the far greater part of them were affected as the girls had been. Except at Kingswood, I have seen no such work of God upon children for above thirty years. [6]

REVIVAL AT CANE RIDGE (AUGUST 6-9, 1801)

In August of 1801, there was a mighty outpouring of the Spirit of God at a place in Kentucky called Cane Ridge. Cane Ridge, one of America's first "camp-meetings," is considered by many to be the most important revival in American history.

At Cane Ridge, the Spirit of God was poured out on "all flesh" as this excerpt clearly shows:

Although only ministers preached prepared sermons, literally hundreds of people became spontaneous exhorters, excitedly giving spiritual advice or tearful warnings. Almost anyone-women, small children, slaves, the shy, the illiterate-could exhort with great effect.

One 7-year-old girl mounted a man's shoulders and spoke wondrous words until she was completely fatigued. When she lay her head on his as if to sleep, someone in the audience suggested "the poor thing" had better be laid down to rest. The girl roused and said, "Don't call me poor, for Christ is my brother, God my father, and I have a kingdom to inherit, and therefore do not call me poor, for I am rich in the blood of the Lamb!" [7]

I love this where it says "literally hundreds of people became spontaneous exhorters." Sounds like the Holy Ghost to me. "Almost anyone-women, small children, slaves, the shy, the illiterate-could exhort with great effect." It sounds like "all flesh" were being used by God. It's wonderful to get a personal word from a man or woman of God that confirms things in your heart, but it's more wonderful for God to use you to exhort or give a word to someone else. There is nothing like the power of God flowing through you to help someone else. Let's not deny our children this blessing of God, using them in a powerful and anointed way to minister to others.

SCOTLAND REVIVAL (1859-1863)

There was a mighty revival in the British Isles from 1859-1863. Children began to minister in a powerful way in this revival.

On Friday 10th June, 1859, a school boy in Coleraine, Northern Ireland, was under such deep conviction of sin that he could not concentrate on his work. His teacher suggested that he ought to go home and pray by himself, and allowed another boy, who had only been converted the day before, to accompany him. On their way they passed an empty house and stopped to pray inside it, where the boy came right through into assurance of salvation. Immediately he insisted on returning to school and announcing; 'Oh, Mr. —, I am so happy; I have the Lord Jesus in my heart.' This affected the whole school in turn, and one by one the boys quietly slipped out of the classroom, and were to be seen kneeling by themselves around the walls of the playground praying silently. The teacher then asked the first boy who had been converted if he would go out and pray with them. When he began to pray for their forgiveness they broke into a bitter cry which penetrated the school, so that the boys remaining inside dropped to their knees and began to cry for mercy. The same thing happened in the girl's school which was upstairs. Parents who called in to collect their children were converted on the spot, ministers were sent for to help counsel and the school was not finally cleared until 11 p.m. that night. [8]

This revival had its origins in the New York prayer meeting started by Jeremiah Lamphier in 1857, from which it had spread across North America sweeping an estimated one million converts into the Kingdom of God, then crossing the Atlantic into Ulster early in 1859, and the rest of the British Isles later in the year, also resulting in a million conversions. In some places people touched by the revival in one place seemed to take it with them into another. At other times Christians heard reports of the movement, and set themselves to pray for a similar visitation, until it arrived spontaneously.

The events in Ireland were widely reported in Scotland. For example, the Scottish Guardian of Tuesday 26th July devotes four and a half columns of small print to the Ulster revival, about one quarter of its total news coverage! This included the following extracts:

From Belfast: On the same twelfth of July the usual bi-weekly meeting of young people was held in the Berry Street church. After an address from Mr. Hanna, a girl about ten years of age was allowed to speak, which she did with affectionate earnestness, and propriety of expression equally remarkable...The meeting, though designed for children was attended by others, and a woman who kept a house of ill fame cried out under strong conviction of sin just as the exercises were concluded. [9]

BELFAST REVIVAL (1859)

It is totally awesome that we see the Spirit of God using children in a leadership role in the same revival—one in Ireland and the other in Scotland. When we look at this revival in Belfast three elements are involved—the children, the Holy Spirit, and the parents. The parents could have stopped the meeting, but they chose not to interfere and to let God move. Mom and Dad, it is so important that you believe the Holy Spirit can use your children just like the parents did at this Belfast Revival.

We are going to see more and more of this in the coming revival. We are going to see God use our children and our youth to minister. Just the other day, I pulled off the internet information about a "Kids On Fire" Prayer Conference for five days in Australia, where all of the speakers are children. Some of you don't believe me, but remember the Bible says, *"Our sons and our daughters will prophesy."*

The meeting was held in a loft on the outskirts of Belfast. A clergyman arrived to find the steps crowded with children, and he helped some of them up. A mother who saw him exclaimed, "Oh no, here's a minister! He'll stop the wee ones." But he assured her that he had come to learn. She told him the meeting had been going on every evening for two months, from 7:30 p.m. till 10. The oldest of the leaders was 13. The minister counted 48 children squatting on the floor, eager and reverent.

At the far end of the loft were benches occupied by 70-80 adults, but it was the children who led. The leader was a boy of thirteen, who prayed with power and conviction, "Show us our mountain of sin, so we can feel You are our Savior from them. Though we are slaves to Satan, yet You,

Jesus, can set us free forever! Loose the bonds of sin, O Jesus, our Deliverer! O Lord, teach us truth and purity. Search all our thoughts, examine our hearts, and show us all the things that are hateful in Your sight! We pray You burn out all our inmost sins and wicked thoughts, against You and against each other. Burn them out, O pure Jesus, but save us in the burning!"

A boy of twelve then tried to teach from Matthew's gospel, but got stuck on the long words, so exhorted instead, "Won't you come to Jesus and be baptized in the Spirit? Oh, come away from the devil and come for Jesus! Prepare the way of the Lord! How many of you are in hell? You know you don't feel free from the devil. Jesus wants to come for you."

Then the clergyman got a shock because the girls began to pray. This offended his traditions but he let the Spirit move. A girl of 17 prayed fervently for the conversion of her family and for forgiveness for all her ingratitude to God. Another, much younger, declared: "I do love Jesus, and I'm not afraid to say what a Savior I've found!"

Then a small girl of about ten arose, frail in body and clothed in rags. Trembling with the Lord's anointing, she raised her hand and proclaimed Jesus crucified for our sins. The power fell instantly. A teenage boy slumped to the floor. Many began to weep. Two or three 12-year olds lay prostrate on the floor. Cries filled the air: "Mercy!

Jesus, can You save me? Help, I'm finished!" Others felt the touch of God's mercy and sang loud praises; tears streaming down their beaming faces.

Finally, well past ten o'clock, the gathering ended with a favorite hymn, "Ye Sleeping Souls Arise," and a very inspired clergyman returned to his hotel praising the Lord. [10]

D. L. MOODY (1837-1899)

D. L. Moody was one of the great evangelists of the 19th century. At the Chicago World's Fair in 1893, over 130,000 people attended Moody's revival meetings in a single day. It is estimated that Moody preached to more than 100 million people in his ministry and won over 1 million souls for the kingdom.

What many do not know about D. L. Moody is that he had a passion for souls of children and young people. Over half of his converts were children. He began his ministry in a little mission Sunday school on North Wells Street in Chicago where he asked to teach a class.

The supply of teachers at that time was in excess of scholars, and the applicant was told that the sixteen teachers were found amply sufficient to instruct twelve children, but they would welcome his services if he could provide his own class. This was exactly to young Moody's taste, and on the following Sunday he arrived at the school leading a procession of eighteen little "hoodlums" that he had gathered. This success made his special calling clear to him, and he continued to gather new scholars for others to teach, feeling that he was not sufficiently gifted for that work himself. [11]

It became clear to Mr. Moody what his calling was—to win children and youth for Jesus Christ. Moody's success continued in an incredible way.

Feeling that his success in the Wells Street Mission pointed to greater undertakings, Mr. Moody, in the fall of 1858, determined to begin another mission school on a larger scale in another part of the city. The same success attended these efforts, and it was soon found that a large hall would be necessary to accommodate the attendance. Such a place was secured in the North Market Hall, a public hall over one of the large city markets of Chicago.

From a description of the building given by Mr. John T. Dale, an early teacher in the school, it was neither attractive in appearance nor clean.

"It was a large, dingy, dilapidated-looking brick building on the outside, while the inside was a great grimy hall with blackened walls and ceiling, and as bare and uninviting as can be imagined. But it was soon crowded to the doors with classes of boys and girls of a type entirely new to me; largely the gamins of the streets, bold, restless, inquisitive youngsters, whose wardrobe was often limited to trousers, shirt, and suspenders—even these in a very advanced stage of decay. The scholars were bubbling over with mischief and exuberance of vitality and sorely tried the patience of the teachers; but the singing was a vent for their spirits, and such singing I had never heard before. The boys who sold papers in the street had an indescribable lung power, and the rest seemed not far behind. There must have been five or six hundred scholars, and it was no easy task to govern such a boisterous crowd, but the teachers seemed to interest their classes, and the exercises passed off with great enthusiasm.

At the close of the school, Mr. Moody took his place at the door and seemed to know personally every boy and girl; he shook hands and had a smile and a cheery word for each one. They crowded about him tumultuously, and his arm must have ached many a time after those meetings. It was easy to see the hold he had on those young lives, and why they were drawn to that place week after week. [12]

The Sunday school mission eventually grew to about 1,500 children and youth. D. L. Moody was still working in secular employment at this time. He did his ministry entirely on the weekend.

There's an interesting story about one of D. L. Moody's childhood converts, Mary Richardson, written by Rev. John Vetter.

In the autumn of 1863, as a home missionary, I was on a tour in northern Michigan. Arriving at the county seat of M— County, I inquired about the gospel needs of the place. There was no meeting house, no preaching. On inquiring about Sunday school, the man, with some hesitation as though not quite certain said, 'Well yes, a Sunday school was started last Sunday by a little girl.' I quickly went to her father's house. Mary was all animation telling me about Mr. Moody and the Sunday school in North Market Hall. Mr. Moody's photograph was hanging on the wall, and another of sixteen street boys with their street names, only one of which I now recall—'Butcher Bill." I must say that I was taken a little by surprise. I had not heard of D. L. Moody at that time. But her face was all aglow as she spoke of the Sunday school in Chicago to which she belonged, and from which she was now so far away. Evidently she had caught Mr. Moody's enthusiasm. Captain Richardson had arrived here with his family but two weeks before, and now a Sunday school is started by this girl in her teens. [13]

CHARLES HADDON SPURGEON (1834-1892)

Charles Haddon Spurgeon was converted at the age of sixteen at a primitive Methodist Church in 1854. At the age of 19, Spurgeon became pastor of the New Park Street Chapel. He was an instant success as pastor and the church exploded with growth. In 1861, the church built a new facility, the Metropolitan Tabernacle, which held 6,000 people. Spurgeon, at 26 years old, was the pastor of one of the first "mega" churches in the world.

Charles Haddon Spurgeon had a heart for reaching children and youth. During his ministry he founded the Stockwell Orphanage which cared for 500 children. Oswald Chambers was converted under Spurgeon's ministry when he was a teenager.

C. H. Spurgeon also wrote a book about children's ministry entitled, *Come Ye Children*. Here are some quotes from that book.

They must be well fed or instructed, because they are in danger of having their cravings perversely satisfied with error. Youth is susceptible to evil doctrine. Whether we teach young Christians truth or not, the devil will be sure to teach them error. They will hear of it somehow, even if they are watched by the most careful guardians. The only way to keep chaff out of the child's little measure is to fill it brimful with good wheat. Oh, that the Spirit of God may help us to do this! The more the young are taught, the better; it will keep them from being misled.

We are specially exhorted to feed them because they

are so likely to be overlooked. I am afraid our sermons often go over the heads of the younger folk—who, nevertheless, may be as true Christians as the older ones. Blessed is he who can so speak as to be understood by a child!

We are specially exhorted to feed the young because this work is so profitable. Do what we may with persons converted late in life, we can never make much of them. We are very glad of them for their own sakes; but at seventy, what remains even if they live another ten years? Train up a child, and he may have fifty years of holy service before him. We are glad to welcome those who come into the vineyard at the eleventh hour, but they have hardly taken their pruning hook and their spade before the sun goes down, and their short day's work is ended. [14]

Whitefield, Wesley, Moody, and Spurgeon all had a passion for the souls of children. It was not beneath these great men of God to take time to minister to them. Where are the great men of God today who have the same passion as Whitfield and Spurgeon?

There are many pastors today with churches of 150 people who are too busy to minister to the children and youth. In America, we are great delegators. Many pastors think, "I'll delegate the youth to the youth pastor and the children to the Sunday school superintendent." But the pastor is the shepherd of the flock. If the pastor doesn't have a heart for children, then his church won't have a heart for children.

JOHN G. LAKE (1870-1935)

John G. Lake was a leader at the Azusa Street Revival and the Pentecostal Outpouring at the turn of the century. He was one of the founding leaders of the Assembly of God.

At the Lake Healing School in Spokane, Washington, 100,000 healings were recorded in five years under John Lake's ministry. Rev. Lake also pastored a large church in South Africa and is credited with bringing revival to that country. The following are a couple of testimonies of how God used children and teens under his ministry.

I was sitting one day in the home of the DeValeras in Krugersdrop, South Africa, when a man arrived who had traveled all over the country. He had been following me from place to place, trying to catch up with me. He suffered a sunstroke, which had affected his mind, and he also had developed a large cancer.

He came into the house and proved to be a friend of the family.

In a little while a six-year-old child who had been sitting near me went across the room, climbed on the man's knees, put her hands on the cancer on his face, and prayed.

I saw the cancer wither. In half an hour, the thing had disappeared. The wound was still there, but in a few days it was healed.

After the child had laid her hands on top of his head, he arose, saying, "Oh! The fire that has been in my brain has gone out," and his mind was normal.

Power belongeth unto God (Ps. 62:11). The simplest soul can touch God and live in the very presence of God and in His power. [15]

Wow! God's power can flow through a six-year-old to heal cancer.

One evening in my own tabernacle, a young girl about 16 to 18 years of age by the name of Hilda suddenly became overpowered by the Spirit of God. She arose and stood on the platform beside me. I recognized at once that the Lord had given the girl a message, so I simply stopped preaching and waited while the Spirit of God came upon her.

She began to chant in some language I did not know, and then made gestures like those a Mohammedan priest would make when chanting prayers.

In the back of the house I observed a young East Indian, whom I knew. He became enraptured and commenced to walk gradually up the aisle. No one disrupted him, and he proceeded up the aisle until he had reached the front. Then he stood looking into the girl's face with intense amazement.

When her message had ceased, I said to him, "What is it?"

He answered, "Oh, she speaks my language!"

I said, "What does she say?"

He came up on the platform beside me and gave the gist of her message:

"She tells me that salvation comes from God. In order to save men, Jesus Christ, Who was God, became man. She says one man cannot save another, that Mohammed was like other men." [16]

Notice the sensitivity of John Lake; he "recognized at once that the Lord had given the girl a message so I simply stopped preaching." How many preachers do you know that would stop in the middle of their sermon and turn their pulpit over to a teenager?

REVIVAL HITS CHINA

H.A. & Josephine Baker were missionaries to China in the 1920's. At the sight of many young boys who were starving to death in the streets, they started an orphanage called Adullam Rescue Mission in Yunnanfu, Yunnan Province of China.

For the most part, these children had been beggars in the streets of the city. In some cases they were poor children with one or both parents dead and had been brought to the Home. There were also some prodigals who had run away from the homes in more distant parts of this or adjoining provinces.

But from whatever source they came, these children, mostly boys ranging in ages from six to eighteen, had come to us without previous training in morals and without education. [17]

Mr. Baker goes on to tell us about the day revival hit at the Adullam Rescue Mission.

The morning prayer meeting was lasting longer than usual. The older children left the room one by one to begin their studies in the school room, while a few of the smaller boys remained on their knees, praying earnestly. The Lord was near. We all felt the presence of the Holy Spirit in our midst. Some who had gone out returned to the room.

Such a mighty conviction of sin—a thing for which we had prayed so long—came to all, that with tears streaming from their eyes and arms uplifted they cried out to the Lord for forgiveness for their sins, which now seemed so black. One after another went down under the mighty power of the Holy Spirit until more than twenty were prostrate on the floor. When I saw that the Lord was doing a most unusual thing in our midst, I went over to the school room and told the boys that if they felt led to come and pray they might be excused from their school work. In a short time, the Chinese teacher was left sitting alone by the table. All his pupils returned to the prayer room, where they were whole-heartedly praying and praising the Lord. When the teacher realized there was nothing for him to do, he started for his home. I had not invited him in with the children, for, although he had been with us a long time, he seemed utter-ly dead, or at least not yet alive to any spiritual understand-ing of the Gospel. Having gone but a short distance from the house, he returned. When he entered the prayer room nobody noticed him, for everyone was intent on his own business with the Lord. The teacher went to the farthest corner of the room, where, for the first time in his life, he knelt down and tried to pray. As the Lord's power was obvi-ous, I felt it best to leave the young man by himself and not to intrude on what I knew must be the work of the Spirit and of the Spirit alone. It was not long before I noticed the teacher with arms uplifted, tears on his face, pleading with the Lord to forgive his sins, which I heard him say were so very, very many. For him to humble himself in this way in the presence of his pupils meant a real Holy Spirit conviction of sin, since he was quite a proud young man. [18]

INDONESIAN REVIVAL (1967-1973)

In the late 1960's and early 1970's, a revival took place in

Indonesia that lasted for years and was marked with many miraculous events. The following is an excerpt from Mel Tari's book *Like a Mighty Wind.*

The Lord moves not only among adults, but also among young people, too—and children. When our teams began to go out from Soe, we had eight groups of children. There were from eight to ten in each group. And the children ranged in age from six to ten. We called them our children's teams.

Every morning they left for school at about 7:00. School lasted from 7:15 to 1:15, when the children went home to eat lunch.

From about 4 to 6 every afternoon, Monday through Friday, these children, instead of playing like most little kids, would get together in prayer meetings. They would kneel, and put their hands together and pray not only for others right around them, but for the whole world. And they would be so concerned that they would weep. Then the Lord would give them perhaps a word of prophecy, or instructions, or reveal something special to them. [19]

BROWNSVILLE REVIVAL 1995 —

On Father's Day in 1995, revival hit at Brownsville Assembly of God. One of the most remarkable traits of this revival is how God is moving powerfully through the youth and the children.

I believe that Brownsville is the beginning of what we are going to see across the entire nation and around the world.

John Kilpatrick

John Kilpatrick is the senior pastor at Brownsville Assembly of God. When John was only 14 years old, he was sitting in a biology class watching a film on dissection, but John's thoughts were on the Lord. John was praying silently to the Lord about getting filled with the Holy Spirit, when it seemed to him that someone lowered the volume on the projector.

Suddenly God spoke to John in an audible voice, "John, this day I have called you to preach My Word. I want you to stay away from the boys and girls in your neighborhood who would be a bad influence on your life."

That same day, God confirmed John's call through his mother. A lady who was selling donuts door to door and did not know John prophesied to his mother the same words God had spoken to him in biology class.

Later in his teenage years, John had a supernatural vision of several angels at an all-night prayer meeting.

Before revival hit at Brownsville, Pastor Kilpatrick was praying and hungering for the God of his childhood. Thank God that Pastor Kilpatrick had the supernatural experiences he had as a teenager, so he knew to pray for them.

The full story of Pastor John Kilpatrick's testimony is found in the book *Feast Of Fire* by John Kilpatrick available through

Brownsville Assembly of God.

Alison Ward

Alison Ward was 19 years old when the revival hit at her home church, Brownsville Assembly. Alison was a typical young person who had grown up in church but had a luke-warm relationship with the Lord. Alison got blasted by the Holy Ghost shortly after the revival started.

On August 18, Alison shared her testimony publicly in front of thousands of people at Brownsville Assembly. Alison shared how God changed her and gave her the gift of intercession. The more Alison shared, the more she began to shake. In response to a question asked by Pastor Kilpatrick, Alison said that many times when she shakes, like she was, that she is inter-ceding for the lost. She can feel what God feels for the lost. Then Alison began to prophecy directly to the lost in the building.

"There's other times whenever I am interceding, it's not painful to my body, but it's painful to my heart, because I know that God loves people so much, and He's in a hurry. He wants everyone… There's not much more time. He aches and grieves for your spirit… He grieves for you."

Pastor Kilpatrick fell under the power and had to be carried to a chair where he stayed for three hours.

Suddenly a spirit of prayer fell on the congregation with the sounds of intercession and groaning for the lost. In a matter of minutes, the altar was full of sinners seeking salvation.

Video tapes of Alison's testimony have circulated around the world. Many churches report that the power of God falls whenever they show the video. I've seen the video personally at least twenty times and every time I see it, it seems like the Holy Ghost is talking directly to me through Alison. I've yet to watch this video testimony without weeping. Praise God, He is moving in a powerful way among our youth and children.

Alison Ward's testimony video is available through Brownsville Assembly of God.

WHAT IS GOD DOING TODAY? (1999-2000+)

God's Spirit is being poured out all over the world like I have never seen before. Children and youth are a major part of this revival. We have seen God moving powerfully in our own meetings with children (which I will talk about later in this book), but right now I want to share some testimonies of others that are "leading children into revival."

John Tasch

John is a friend of mine who has been involved in children and youth ministry for more than 25 years. John was the children's pastor at Victory Christian Center in Tulsa, Oklahoma, for ten years. Currently John and Shirley Tasch are taking children on missions trips around the world. This is one testimony that John shared at our annual National Children's Pastors

Conference in Minneapolis.

"Jesus said, *'Go into all the world and preach the gospel to every creature. And these signs will follow those that believe.'* For the past seven years we've been taking children all over the world. What do they do? They preach, they teach, and they lay hands on the sick. I step back and watch.

"Children are laying hands on people in wheelchairs. Once in Mexico, I preached to 550 people, telling them how God wanted to set people free and heal them. When I asked those who need healing to raise their hands, about 200 hands went up. I said to the kids, 'Begin to pray for those who have their hands raised.' I stood behind the pulpit and watched as a 9-year-old boy yanked a lady up out of a wheelchair. She could not walk. He kept on pulling and pulling until he finally got her up...and she walked! We've also seen blind eyes opened and demons cast out in our services."

Vann Lane

Vann Lane is another close friend whom God has raised up to help lead children into revival. Vann is the children's pastor at Brownsville Assembly of God in Pensacola, Florida. Vann shared this testimony at our NCPC conference in 1998.

"I have some kids in children's church who are like fire

hoses with absolutely no resistance at all. At 10 years of age, Jacob Green could be found under the pews, face in the carpet, seeking God, while everyone else was socializing. Jacob knew God. That same year, he began to minister in children's church because I needed an elder. I pray for the children for colds and scrapes, but for 'tough' cases, I get Jacob.

"Jacob laid hands on a girl who was legally blind. He said, 'Lord, You've opened the eyes of the blind, why not these?' The little girl with thick glasses walked out the door reading a fine-print Bible and left her glasses on the altar. She never came back for them! Healing flowed through the hands of a child—there was nothing to hinder the flow. Children were challenged and they rose to the challenge."

David Walters

Another friend, David Walters, has been having Holy Ghost meetings with children and youth for over 15 years. David has been a pioneer of a new kind of children's ministry. The following is an excerpt from David's book, *Kids In Combat.*

"A number of years ago we were ministering at a family camp in Ohio. We were given responsibility for the teenagers. Another minister was speaking to the children, and another was ministering to the adults. We found that many of the teenagers were not interested in spiritual things and were resisting the Holy Spirit. Although we had made some progress with them after two days, it was still an uphill battle.

"We decided to ask if we could minister to the younger children the next afternoon. We had a group of about thirty children between the ages of five and ten. I shared the salvation message with them, prayed for some who wanted to surrender to Christ and prayed for the remainder of them to receive the baptism of the Holy Spirit. Then we simply sat down and waited.

"After a period of time some of them began to weep and confess their sins. Some fell down under the power of the Spirit, and a six-year-old boy had a very detailed prophetic vision of America.

"When we were finally finished, we asked the youngsters to walk up the hill to the main building where the adults were staying. Halfway up the hill, the children caught up with the teenagers, and the Holy Spirit began to move upon them as well! This resulted in their falling down on the ground with tears of repentance. We were already in the sanctuary because we had driven our car, and we were listening to the musicians arranging songs for the meeting that evening. The guest minister was also there preparing his evening message.

"Suddenly the doors burst open, and the children and

teenagers came pouring in. As soon as they did, the Holy Spirit fell on the adults! People began to laugh, weep and get healed and delivered. Some danced while others shouted and praised. Needless to say, the musicians were not able to sing their prepared songs that night, and the guest speaker never delivered his message! This revival lasted for two days!" [20]

1 Mark Galli, *Christian History Magazine* Vol. XII, No 2, (Carol Stream, Illinois: Christianity Today, Inc., 1993), pp. 20.

2 Harry S. Stout *Christian History Magazine* Vol. XII, No 2, (Carol Stream, Illinois: Christianity Today, Inc., 1993), p. 10.

3 Harry Sprange, *Children In Revival Kingdom Kids,* (Scotland, Great Britain: Christian Focus Publications Ltd, 1994), pp. 14, 15.

4 Sprange, p. 19.

5 *Christian History Magazine* Vol. XII, No 2, (Carol Stream, Illinois: Christianity Today, Inc., 1993), p. 2.

6 David Walters, *Children Aflame,* (Taylors, South Carolina: Faith Printing Company, reprint 1996), pp. 10—11, 24.

7 Mark Galli, *Christian History Magazine* Vol. XIV, No 1, (Carol Stream, Illinois: Christianity Today, Inc., 1993), p. 14.

8 This is recorded in full in John Carson's *'God's River In Spate'* pages 35—36 and together with many other anecdotes about children in Henry Montgomery's 'The Children in '59'.

9 Sprange, pp. 86, 87.

10 *Revival Fires: Revival In Belfast, The Meeting Of The Wee Ones,* (Dublin, Ireland:,1860).

11 William R. Moody, *The Life of D. L. Moody by His Son,* (Murfreesboro, Tennessee: Sword of the Lord Publishers, reprint), p. 55.

12 Moody, pp. 56,57.

13 Moody, p. 60.

14 C. H. Spurgeon, *Come Ye Children,* (Pasadena, Texas: Pilgrim Publications), pp. 79.

15 John G. Lake, *Adventures In God,* (Tulsa, Oklahoma: Harrison House, Inc., 1981), pp. 15, 16.

16 Lake, pp. 21, 22.

17 H. A. Baker, *Visions Beyond The Veil,* (Monroeville, Pennsylvania: Whitaker Books, 1973), p. 11.

18 Baker, pp. 21, 22.

19 Mel Tari, *Like A Mighty Wind,* (Carol Stream, Illinois, Creation House, reprint 1972), p. 51.

20 David Walters, *Kids In Combat,* (Macon, Georgia: Good News Fellowship Ministries, 1989), pp. 55, 56.

CHAPTER THREE

Be In Revival Yourself

Then Peter said unto them, Repent, and be baptized every one of you in the name of Jesus Christ for the remission of sins, and ye shall receive the gift of the Holy Ghost. For the promise is unto you, and to your children, and to all that are afar off, even as many as the Lord our God shall call.
—*Acts 2:38-39*

Obedience without relationship is legalism. Relationship without obedience is hypocrisy. The two things that will cause your kids to run from God are legalism and hypocrisy.

It's important that we obey God, however, our obedience must spring from a passionate love relationship with Jesus Christ. In other words, we obey God because we want to, not because we have to.

There are hundreds of books on child training and discipline, teaching us as parents to train our children to be good. However, this book intends to focus on the one aspect of child training that is left out many times—how to teach your children to be on fire for God. Don't misunderstand me—God expects our kids to be obedient and well behaved, but He wants them to obey because they are in love with Him.

JUMP IN THE RIVER

If we want our children to be passionate for God then we must be on fire for God. If we want our youth to be flowing in the revival, then it's important that Mom and Dad flow in the revival and that you attend a church that is flowing in revival.

I believe that the church and home are the most powerful influences in the lives of our children. If their parents and their church are on fire for God, then they will be too.

We all learn by following the lead of others, following the examples of our leaders. I remember the first time I attended a Pentecostal church. I didn't know how to worship God, even after I got saved. I loved God but didn't know how to worship Him. I learned to worship God by watching other people worship God. I remember the first Sunday I lifted my hands, but not too high (about belly-button level.) The next week I lifted my hands up to my chest. Finally I was lifting them as high as I could above my head.

Children and youth learn the same way—by following the examples of others, especially their parents, their church, and their peers. If you look up the word "example" in the dictionary it means "something worthy of imitation." That's how children learn—by imitation.

In 1979, I was helping a pastor pioneer a church in Port Huron, Michigan. One Sunday morning, we had a Holy Ghost service. On this particular Sunday, one little girl named Jennifer (she was 2½ years old) went home and gathered all of her dolls from around the house. She stood all the dolls up along the wall in her bedroom and layed hands on and prayed for each doll. Next, Jennifer knocked her dolls over on the floor, then she went by and put little handkerchiefs over their dresses.

What was Jennifer doing? She was imitating. Is this a good thing? Yes, because children learn by imitating. Your children are imitating your good traits and your bad traits.

When my son, Mark, was learning to talk we began to teach him to say "please" instead of just demanding things. When he would ask for the potatoes at dinnertime, we would respond by saying, "How do you ask?" Mark would say, "Please." We were hoping he would catch the revelation of saying "please" without us reminding him, but it didn't seem to happen.

One day, I had a ball in my hand. Mark said, "Dad-Ball," which meant he wanted the ball.

I said, "How do you ask?"

He responded by saying, "Please?" I handed Mark the ball; he looked at me and said, "Thank you." I was in shock. We hadn't taught him to say "thank you" yet. We were still working on "please."

I thought to myself, "Where did he learn to say thank you?" Then it hit me, he was imitating me. If I asked him to do something and he obeyed, I would say, "Thank you." But I rarely would say "please" when asking him to do things.

Here's my point–children will naturally do what you do with very little resistance because God programmed children to learn by imitation.

It is impossible to lead your children into revival if you are not in revival yourself. You can do everything else correctly concerning discipline and child training, but the only way your child will be passionately in love with Jesus Christ is if you are on fire for God yourself.

This was true in my own family. My father was a good, hardworking man, but he was married and divorced three times. Yet I'm a believer today because my dad got saved when I was sixteen years old.

I was a junior in high school, I had hair down past my shoulders, and I was very much involved in the drug scene of the 70's.

My junior year in high school was the worst year of my life. In the fall of that year (1975) I was arrested for selling drugs. My friend and I were handcuffed, read our rights, and taken to the police station. They gave me a phone to call my parents. On the telephone where the phone number was supposed to be it said, "Good-bye, suckers." My father came to pick me up, and he was not very happy.

A few months later, my friends and I were skipping classes and getting drunk. I was driving my car in front of our high school, trying to show off. I took a turn pretty fast and lost control of my car and hit a tree which snapped when the car hit it. My friend and I both went through the windshield and almost killed ourselves. The security guard who watched the high school parking lot, said to me, "You're a very lucky young man. If the tree had not snapped you would have been dead."

It was during this time, in the spring of 1976, that my brothers and I came home from school and found my dad home early from work. (I had three brothers who were just like me.) My dad said to us, "Boys, I want to talk to you." We all sat down in the living room wondering what was up. Immediately, I thought my dad had found some of my drugs or something. But instead of chewing us out, Dad began to read from John chapter nine about the man who was born blind.

This was strange. I couldn't remember my dad ever reading from the Bible. After telling us the story of how Jesus healed the blind man, he closed his Bible and said, "Boys, I want to tell you something. I believe that Jesus still heals today, and I want you to know that God has healed my back." (My dad had had a bad back for years.)

My brothers and I looked at one another. We thought, "Our dad has flipped his lid." My father went on to tell us his testimony.

My dad was a stockbroker. He was at his office and a total stranger came in and said, "God told me to come in here and sell my stock." At the end of their conversation, she asked my dad, "Is there anything I can pray with you about?" My father replied, "I've had a bad back for years." She prayed for my dad's back and left. Shortly after she left, my father felt this warm glow in his back. The heat became so intense that he could not concentrate anymore, so he left work and came home. To make a long story short, God healed my dad's back and my dad got saved. He began to go to church every Sunday. One Sunday he asked me to come along with him. It was wild! People were clapping and shouting. They would lift their hands during worship, speak in tongues and prophesy. There has been a lot of emphasis recently about being seeker-sensitive in churches and not offending the unbeliever, but what got my attention was that this church was weird.

I had never seen anything like it and even though I was uncomfortable, I could tell that these people were sincere and that they loved God.

It took a while, but six months later, I followed my dad into revival. I was born again on September 12, 1976. The thing that got my attention more than anything else was that I watched my Dad change right before my very eyes. I had a new dad.

My father was not the perfect father. He did a lot of things right and a lot of things wrong, but he did do the one thing right that really mattered. He got saved and filled with the Holy Ghost, and he fell in love with Jesus Christ.

More than anything else I serve God today because of my father. My point is this, Mom and Dad, you don't have to be perfect. Your kids, especially if they are teenagers, know that you aren't perfect, but if you are in love with Jesus, they will be in love with Jesus. If you are excited about church, they will be excited about church. If you are on fire for God, they will be on fire for God.

I heard it said to men that the best thing you can do for your children is to love your wife. I almost agree with that statement, however, I believe that the best things you can do for your children is to be passionately in love with Jesus Christ and express that love in a way that is visible to your kids. This is why I believe that it is so important that families worship together at church and at home. (We will discuss more about worship in chapter six.)

CHAPTER FOUR

You Get What You Believe

In I Samuel chapter three, we read the story about how God spoke to the child Samuel.

I SAMUEL 3:1-14

1 And the child Samuel ministered unto the Lord before Eli. And the word of the Lord was precious in those days; there was no open vision.

2 And it came to pass at that time, when Eli was laid down in his place and his eyes began to wax dim, that he could not see;

3 And ere the lamp of God went out in the temple of the Lord, where the ark of God was, and Samuel was laid down to sleep;

4 That the Lord called Samuel: and he answered, Here am I.

5 And he ran unto Eli, and said, Here am I; for thou calledst me. And he said, I called not; lie down again. And he went and lay down.

6 And the Lord called yet again, Samuel. And Samuel arose and went to Eli, and said, Here am I; for thou didst call me. And he answered, I called not, my son; lie down again.

7 Now Samuel did not yet know the Lord, neither was the word of the Lord yet revealed unto him.

8 And the Lord called Samuel again the third time. And he arose and went to Eli, and said, Here am I; for thou didst call me. And Eli perceived that the Lord had called the child.

9 Therefore Eli said unto Samuel, Go, lie down: and it shall be, if he call thee, that thou shalt say, Speak, Lord; for thy servant heareth. So Samuel went and lay down in his place.

10 And the Lord came, and stood, and called as at other times, Samuel, Samuel. Then Samuel answered, Speak; for thy servant heareth.

11 And the Lord said to Samuel, Behold, I will do a thing in Israel, at which both the ears of every one that heareth it shall tingle.

12 In that day I will perform against Eli all things which I have spoken concerning his house: when I begin, I will also make an end.

13 For I have told him that I will judge his house for ever for the iniquity which he knoweth; because his sons made themselves vile, and he restrained them not.

14 And therefore I have sworn unto the house of Eli, that the iniquity of Eli's house shall not be purged with sacrifice nor offering forever.

There is a lot of revelation for parents and teachers in this story about Samuel. First of all this story is biblical proof that God does use children in a powerful way. I'm still amazed at how many parents and even preachers don't believe that God can use children in a supernatural way when the Bible has many stories of God using kids and teenagers.

Ask yourself these questions: Is the Bible the Word of God? Do you believe the Bible is true? Does God use children in the gifts of the Spirit such as prophecy, word of wisdom, gifts of healings, and working of miracles?

If you answered "yes" to the first two questions, then you should have no problem answering "yes" to the third question, because the Bible has many stories of God using kids and youth, for example, Samuel, David, Daniel, and the three Hebrew children.

Let's take a closer look at this story of Samuel. In chapter one of I Samuel, we see that Hannah was barren; she had no children. One day Hannah went to the temple and poured out her heart to God. Hannah made a promise to God that if He would give her a son, she would give him to the Lord for the ministry. God answered Hannah's prayer. She conceived and gave birth to a strong, healthy boy. Hannah named him Samuel, which means "asked of God."

When Samuel was weaned (my guess would be between the ages of 2-4), Hannah brought him to the temple and gave him to Eli to train for the ministry. Who knows what Eli thought of this-maybe he thought Hannah was trying to get free day care! This was not an easy thing for Hannah to do, but Hannah was very determined about keeping her promise to God.

This brings us to the story in chapter three where God speaks to Samuel. God spoke to Samuel four times before Samuel was able to receive the word from God. Why did God have to speak four times? Was it the will of God for Samuel to hear the first time? Of course it was. If God is calling you by name, I think it's pretty clear that He wants to talk to you. So why did God have to speak four times? What happened between the third time and the fourth time?

Verse 7 is very enlightening. It says, *"Now Samuel did not yet know the Lord, neither was the word of the Lord revealed to him."*

This tells me that Eli was not doing a good job as Samuel's teacher because Samuel did not really know the Lord yet and he hadn't been taught to hear from God. Hannah brought Samuel to the temple for the express purpose of being trained in ministry, but Eli wasn't doing his part. I think the reason that Eli didn't teach Samuel about these things was because he thought, like a lot of adults do, that children can't be used by God until they "grow up."

Let's take a closer look at verses 8 and 9: *"And the Lord called Samuel again the third time. And he arose and went to Eli and said, "Here am I, for you did call me. And Eli perceived that the Lord had called the child. Therefore Eli said unto Samuel,*

Go, lie down: and it shall be, if he call then that you shalt say, Speak, Lord; for the servant heareth."

Notice in verse 8 it says, *"Eli perceived the Lord had called."* I believe that is the first time Eli thought, "Hey! Maybe God's talking to you, Samuel."

Here's my point: Samuel did not receive the word from God until his teacher believed that he could.

There are three individuals involved in this story: God, the teacher, and the child. It took all three to "have faith" before Samuel received.

It is also very important that parents believe that God can use their children.

Willie George is one of my spiritual fathers. I'm doing what I'm doing today because Willie influenced my life 20 years ago when I was attending Rhema Bible Training Center in Tulsa, Oklahoma.

One day I asked Willie, "Why is it so hard for parents to believe that their own children can step out into the supernatural and be used in the gifts of the Spirit?" (Many times I had more faith in their children than they did. This seemed odd to me.)

I never forgot what Willie said: "It's because most parents know their children after the flesh."

Wow! Now I understood. Even Jesus "could not do any mighty works" in His hometown. Why? Because they knew Him after His flesh. They had no understanding of the call on

His life or the gift of God in Him.

Mom and Dad, don't look at your children after the flesh; look for the gift of God in them. Some of your children are called to be apostles, prophets, evangelists and pastors.

The following is a quote from Clarine Chun's book *Please Do Not Despise Me.* Clarine and her husband pastor a church in Malaysia.

The church is constantly expected to provide a program to keep their kids happy while Daddy and Mommy are in the worship service. Parents also have this mentality that their kids cannot understand the pastor's message, therefore they need to be taken out of the service. Sometimes, I wonder when parents and adults are going to allow their children's spiritual maturity to catch up and be on par with their level of intellectual development.

It all has to start with our thinking. Why do you send your child for swimming lessons? Because you believe he's going to make it. Surely no parent will send his/her child for swimming lessons anticipating the child to drown. Why do you send your child to art classes? Because you believe (with all the mess he will make) that he will learn art. Why do we keep kids in an adult worship service? Because we believe in their spiritual abilities.

Currently, in my own church, once our church children are past kindergarten age they are not allowed in the nursery. Many of them opt to stay in the adult worship service anyway. These kids do not run around, play, or do coloring in the service. Instead, they sit down, listen to the preacher, take notes of the sermon, and respond to the altar call.

If our children can sit in school for six hours every day and are expected by both teachers and parents to give their full concentration, why can't we expect that they will also sit for two hours and join the adult service?

The problem lies with parents and their inability to believe that their children can do it. Parents have this concept—how can we expect our children to identify and understand what the pastor is saying?

Currently, new-born babies in our church are encouraged to stay in the adult service. The six-year-olds and above take notes of what the pastor is preaching. They respond to the altar calls together with the adults. They pray, worship, tithe, weep, laugh, speak in tongues, and get slain in the Spirit together with their daddies and mommies. I am very strict with the children and train them to understand that they too are part of the body of Christ. The adult service is not complete without them.

We hardly have problems with children crying, playing, and running all over in our church. We believe in them. Children will be what you believe them to be. By the time the children join the youth group, they are ready for leadership.

The praise and worship ministers in our church are a mixture of young and old. The youngest, Ai Ling, started when she was eleven years old.

I do not run Superkids Church at the same time as the adult worship service. The adult service is from 9:00 to 12:00 p.m. Superkids Church is from 4:00 to 6:00 p.m. This gives me the advantage of having quality musicians for Superkids Church. As you know, if the services run simultaneously, all your good musicians will be in the adult service. This arrangement also means that my teachers do not have to go on a rotation basis. This gives us a strong bond in the teacher-student relationship.

Since we are training an army, we must be willing to make sacrifices even if it means coming back to church after the morning service. There is a great fulfillment among the teachers because the fruits speak for themselves. [1]

Clarine's story brings me to another point: pastors and church leaders need to make church more inclusive for teenagers and children. There should be times when kids, teens, and adults are taught separately, but there also needs to be times when families worship God together, especially if the Spirit of God is moving. We need to communicate to our youth and our children that they are a vital part of the church. I believe very strongly that the youth and children should be part of the worship team and ministries in the church.

This is one reason why I was so impressed with the revival at Brownsville. They made room for their children and youth. I believe that is why so many youth and children have been impacted in such a powerful way at the Brownsville Revival.

In Mark 11:23 we read a very familiar scripture, *"For verily I say unto you, That whosoever shall say unto this mountain, Be thou removed, and be thou cast into the sea; and shall not doubt in his heart, but shall believe that those things which he saith shall come to pass he shall have whatsoever he saith."*

The main thought of this scripture is that you get what you believe for and say with your mouth. If your children are not passionately in love with Jesus, maybe you need to change what you are believing about them and change what you are saying about them.

You can start the change right now. Take a few moments and ask God to forgive you for not believing that He can work through children. Then start to say things like:

> *Father, I pray for (your child's name) that his/her foot steps are ordered by You. Every time that _____ sins or takes a step towards the world, I pray that the Holy Spirit will convict him/her of sin. _____ is passionately in love with Jesus Christ. _____ is hungry for the things of God. God has a plan for _____ 's*

life. God wants to use _____ in a powerful way.

Pray this way for your children every day for one month and it will change how you think about your kids.

1 Clarine Chun, *Please Do Not Despise Me,* (Kedah, West Malaysia, Trinity Baptist Church, reprint 1996), pp. 67-68, 78-79.

CHAPTER FIVE

Expose Your Children and Youth to Revival

And, all people served the Lord all the days of Joshua, and all the days of the elders that outlived Joshua, who had seen all the great works of the Lord, that he did for Israel... and there arose another generation after them, which knew not the Lord, nor yet the works which he had done for Israel. And the children of Israel did evil in the sight of the Lord, and served Baalim:

—Judges 2:7-11

"The generation that has never seen a display of God's power is more likely to go the way of the world than the generation that has witnessed such a mighty work."

—Arthur Wallis

It is vital that our youth and children be exposed to revival if we want them to be passionate for Jesus. Many times, parents and even pastors will think it is easier to have a move of God without the children, but this is a grave mistake.

Many years ago, I was attending a healing crusade with about two thousand people in attendance. Before the meeting began the crusade director made an announcement, "We don't want any children to be seated in the first ten rows because we don't want to disturb the anointing of God." I was in shock! I wasn't a parent at the time, but if I did have children I would have wanted them to sit right in the middle of the anointing of God. It is attitudes like that that push our children away from a love relationship with Jesus.

Don't misunderstand me. I believe strongly that parents need to train their children to sit and respect what God is doing in the service. If babies are getting fussy, then it's right for their parents to take them outside to quiet them down.

It seems like an easy solution just to provide entertainment for the children, but we are sacrificing our children and the future of the revival if we take this approach.

In today's world, it is vital that our teens and children be exposed to the power of God. If revival breaks out at your church, make a way to include the youth and the kids. One experience with the Holy Ghost can change their life forever.

I was saved September 12, 1976, when I was 17 years old. In May of 1976, my father remarried a lady who was a born-again Christian.

My stepmom had a daughter named Madeline, who was 14 years old. After my dad got saved and I got saved, I saw all three of my brothers get saved, but I never saw Madeline go forward to an altar call.

My step-sister, Madeline, was kind of sitting on the fence. She went to church because her mom made her go, but at school she wasn't living for the Lord.

In August of 1977, my family attended a Full Gospel Business Men's Convention in Detroit, Michigan. One of the speakers was an evangelist named Jim Spillman. One night they asked Jim Spillman to minister to the young people. There were about 200 teenagers in attendance in the youth meeting; about 100 were from the same church so we all knew one another.

Jim preached for about 10 minutes and then he began to flow in prophecy and the word of knowledge. He began to call teenagers up to the front and read their mail, right in front of everybody.

It got quiet in there real quick. We knew that God was there and we had better be good. After delivering the "words" Jim would lay hands on the youth and they would fall under the power. Teenagers were lying on the floor everywhere. We had never seen anything like this in a youth service.

I was sitting next to my step-sister, Madeline. She was praying quietly to herself, "Lord, please don't let him call me up there." Madeline kept praying over and over, "Lord, please don't let him call me up there."

Finally, Jim pointed at Madeline, "This little blonde girl, come up here." Madeline's prayer changed as she walked to the front. Now she prayed, "Lord, please don't let him touch me." (She didn't want to fall under the power.)

I'll never forget what happened next. Madeline stood right in front of Jim Spillman. (She's praying to herself, "Lord, please don't let him touch me.") Jim pointed at Madeline and said, "Now, honey, I have specific instructions from the Lord not to touch you." God answered Madeline's prayer.

That night changed Madeline's life; she started serving God after that. Our children and youth need this! It's not an option! They need to be exposed to the power of God! They need to be exposed to revival.

Years ago, I was praying and talking to God. I asked the Lord, "Why is it that so many children who are raised in church, have good parents, and learn the memory verses every week, fall away from God when they hit their teen years or go off to college?"

The Holy Ghost spoke to my heart, "One reason is that many of them have never had an experience with the Holy Ghost." Our teens know that drugs are real, sex is real, but they don't know that God's power is real. This is why we lose so many of our kids. This is why it's so important that we expose our children to revival, because one experience with the Holy Ghost can change their life forever.

Think about Saul of Tarsus. He was in the business of persecuting and killing Christians. One day, while Saul was on the road to Damascus he had an experience with the Holy Ghost. Saul was knocked off his horse and was blinded for days.

Saul was not blind because of sickness, but because of the

power of God. That day changed his life. Saul of Tarsus became the Apostle Paul. Every time he got up to preach his sermon was, "I was on the road to Damascus." What happened on the road to Damascus? Paul had an experience with the Holy Ghost and it changed his life.

Another reason to expose children to revival is so they can participate in the spirit of repentance that is predominate at most revivals.

Repentance is key to revival. Revival began for me when I began to repent of my pride and let God touch me.

It is also important for kids to see Mom and Dad repent. Your kids know that you're not perfect. It helps them to open up to God when they see you repenting. I think it is especially important for children to see their father weeping at the altar. Many times in revival services and watching revival videos, tears will come to my eyes, or a spirit of repentance will come on me. When my son, Mark, Jr. (who is 12 at the time of this writing) sees that, he will come hug me, or start praying for me. This brings us closer together and is healthy for our relationship.

The Bible says that in the lasts days, He will turn the hearts of the fathers to the children and the hearts of the children to the fathers. How can this happen if families are always separated at church?

The Spirit of God has instructed me to conduct Family Revival Services. We have everybody—parents, teens, and kids—together for a powerful time of worship, preaching, and ministry. I don't do any puppets or drama, maybe an object lesson or two. God always shows up in a powerful way.

For years we have had Holy Ghost services at camp, but when the children came home, Mom and Dad had no idea how to nurture what happened to their children at camp. The Spirit of God spoke to me and said, "It's time to stop hiding your ministry. You need to have revival services in front of the entire church."

In October of 1998, we hosted the Minnesota Children's Revival Service. There were 600 parents and children who attended from churches all across the state. This revival service was a tremendous success. It was a confirmation of what the Lord wants to do. Our vision is to conduct this type of service all across the country and challenge children to reach their schools for Jesus.

CHAPTER SIX

Worship at Church and at Home

"Too often the children have been ignored in the present resurgence of praise and worship. They are often shuttled off to a film room or a game room somewhere on the premises while the adults enjoy their worship experience. If this continues, our revival of worship will perish with us." —Judson Cornwall

MATTHEW 21:16
...And Jesus saith unto them, Yea; have you never read, Out of the mouth of babes and sucklings thou hast perfected praise?

One thing about worship is that it is a universal language. Worship transcends all generations and all cultures. Toddlers and even little babies will respond to anointed praise and worship. If an up-beat praise song begins in church, toddlers will naturally start dancing to the beat of the music. (It takes an adult to teach them not to dance in church.)

I believe this is one thing that Jesus meant when He said in Matthew 19:14, *"Except you change and become like little chil-*

dren you will not enter the kingdom of heaven." Jesus told us we need to change and become like children. In other words, there is much that little children can teach us about praise and worship, but how can we learn if we are never together for praise and worship?

I am not advocating that we never have children's church or youth group worship services. I believe we need both. There needs to be a time when families worship together, and there should be a time when children and youth have their own worship services.

I was talking to a friend of mine, Greg Permann, who is Children's Pastor at Community Bible Church in Fergus Falls, Minnesota. (Greg is the pastor of the children I mentioned in the introduction of this book. I've never seen children worship like Greg's kids.)

Greg mentioned to me that some of the parents in the church would ask for prayer because their children just weren't worshiping in the adult services. Greg was surprised because they worshiped really well in children's church. (It was easier for the children to learn how to worship in children's church because they felt intimidated in the adult service. I think many times kids think that the service isn't directed to them so they click out or maybe they feel intimidated by the bigness of it.)

This tells me three things:

    1. We need to have children's church worship services because it is easier for kids to worship in those settings.

2. Pastors and worship leaders need to do a better job of including teens and kids in the worship services by communicating that praise and worship is for them, and have teens and kids be part of the worship team.

3. Parents need to have a praise and worship time at home. This doesn't have to be a thing like we will worship every day at 8:00 a.m. In fact, I think it's better if it's spontaneous. One of my favorite praise songs right now is the "Happy Song."[1] Every once in a while I put on that CD and dance around the house with Deb and the kids. Many times I'm more free to dance at home than at church. What I'm saying is that this helps me to get free in worship as much as it helps my kids.

A Personal Revival

One thing that happened to me at the revival in Toronto was the Holy Ghost showed me how my pride and judgmental attitude toward others was affecting my worship and personal relationship with God.

When I went to my first service at the Toronto Airport Christian Fellowship, I was there because I was hungry for God and I wanted to go somewhere where nobody knew me.

The Bible says in Luke 3:16 that Jesus will baptize us with the Holy Ghost and fire. I had been baptized with the Holy Ghost back in 1976, so I was familiar with that experience, but

I never understood about being baptized with fire. What did that mean? To be honest, this was one of the scriptures I stayed away from. I wanted the Holy Ghost, but I wasn't sure about the "fire stuff."

One thing about fire is that it can be a blessing or a destroyer. If you were camping outside in a tent on a cool night, you could make a little campfire. You could come around that campfire and warm yourself up. It would be a blessing to you. However, if you were a log next to the fire and someone picked you up and put you on the fire, that same fire would become a destroyer.

In a similar way, if you are in the right place with God, fire is a blessing; it warms you. If you are not in the right place with God, that same fire can be a destroyer, not to destroy you, but to destroy the things that are displeasing to God.

At Toronto, the praise and worship was awesome. The preaching was great. The preacher, Mark Dupont, gave a call to pray for pastors. I went forward to be prayed for. (Understand that at this time in my life, I rarely would get in a line to be prayed for and I had never fallen under the power, even though I had been a Pentecostal Christian for almost 20 years.)

As I was getting prayed for, I began to feel a little dizzy, but I didn't fall, laugh or have any manifestation. Bill, who was praying for me, prayed for about 20 minutes. At one point I started to fall forward, so I pulled myself back; and then I started to fall back, so I pulled myself forward, kind of like a teeter totter. Eventually I just collapsed on the floor because I couldn't stand up any more.

I started to get up and then Bill came back, prayed for me again, and I fell down again. Finally I just layed there for about an hour. It was like a Holy Ghost operation time for me.

I didn't laugh, cry, shake, or have any unusual manifestation, but what happened to me changed my life forever. It all happened on the inside of me. The Holy Ghost began to talk to me about my worship. At this time in my life I never danced, shouted, or jumped up and down during worship. I liked quiet worship. My favorite worship scripture was, "Be still and know that I am God."

My attitude was that it was okay for others to dance, but "that's not for me." The Holy Ghost showed me that the real reason that I didn't dance or shout was because of my pride. I was concerned about what others would think of me.

There is a song they would sing in Toronto that went like this: "Shout to the Lord, shout to the Lord; it breaks the heavy yoke when you shout to the Lord."

I began to do just that when I worshiped. I began to shout to the Lord and dance to the Lord, and when I did, that yoke of pride was broken. It seemed like I could feel it just roll off when I began to shout.

Another thing the Holy Ghost nailed me on in Toronto was a judgmental, critical attitude toward others and how they worshiped God. One night during the worship, there was a lady right in front of me who had a piece of Christmas garland in her hand. She was waving it back and forth, and it was really bugging me. Normally if someone was doing something that bugged me during worship, I would look the other way. But this lady was really tall, and her arms blocked my view of the overhead.

We were singing the song, "We Will Dance On Streets That Are Golden." It was a really anointed worship service. It seemed like everyone around me was loving on Jesus and really flowing in worship except for me; I'm flowing in heavy judgement. I almost tapped her on the shoulder and said, "Would you stop doing that?" (I'm very glad that I didn't.) For one second, I stopped looking at the Christmas garland and I looked at her face. Tears were streaming down her face as she worshiped Jesus. The Lord spoke to me three little words, "She loves Me."

I immediately broke and began to weep. "Forgive me, Lord, for being so judgmental." As soon as I repented of being judgmental, I was free to worship. I didn't realize how my judgmental and critical attitude was affecting my worship and relationship with God.

I know that this testimony does not paint me in a very good light. It is always hard to confess your sins publicly, however I find that it helps people when you are transparent with them. Every time I share this testimony publicly, I always have someone, (usually a man) come up to me and tell how it helped them. They have struggled with the same pride and judgment issues.

SETTING AN EXAMPLE

I've noticed in most children's ministries where I've ministered, the girls enter into worship easier than the boys. It is the same all over the world, no matter what country or culture. Many times the boys will just sit there while the girls are going for it. Why is this? Could it be that the boys struggle with worship because their fathers have a hard time entering in?

Men, if you want your children to be in love with Jesus, then they need to see your love for Jesus. Don't let pride stop you from entering into praise and worship. Not only will you "get free," but you will help your sons to get free also.

MATTHEW 21:12-16

12 And Jesus went into the temple of God, and cast out all them that sold, and bought in the temple, and overthrew the tables of the moneychangers, and the seats of them that sold doves.

13 And said unto them, It is written, My house shall be called the house of prayer; but ye have made it a den of thieves.

14 And the blind and the lame came to him in the temple; and he healed them.

15 And when the chief priests and scribes saw the wonderful things that he did, and the children crying in the temple, and saying, Hosanna to the son of David; they were sore displeased,

16 And said unto him, Hearest thou what these say? And Jesus saith unto them, Yea; have ye never read, Out of the mouth of babes and sucklings thou hast perfected praise?

In this story, Jesus went into the temple, turned over the tables of the moneychangers and kicked them out of the temple. Then he healed the sick and the lame, and the children began to praise Him.

Now look at verse 15 again: *"And when the chief priests and scribes saw the wonderful things that he did, and the children crying in the temple, and saying, Hosanna to the son of David; they were sore displeased."*

What really got the Pharisees mad was that the children were worshiping Jesus. Look at what these children were saying, "Hosanna to the son of David." That doesn't sound like kid talk to me. Where did these kids learn how to worship God like this?

Let's look back at verse 9 which talks about the triumphal entry into Jerusalem, what we know as Palm Sunday.

MATTHEW 21:9
And the multitudes that went before, and that followed, cried, saying, Hosanna to the son of David: Blessed is he that cometh in the name of the Lord; Hosanna in the highest.

What were these children doing? They were imitating what

they had seen their mom and dad doing just a few hours earlier. This is why it is so important for children to be with mom and dad during worship service and for families to worship God together at home.

There are many different ways to enter into praise and worship. Let me encourage you to worship at home. Don't just talk about these things with kids, but actually do them. Have the children do the different types of praise and worship as you talk about them. Of course you need to do them too. (One of my pet peeves in children's church was when a parent would come in to help and then sit there like a bump on a log during worship. They would click out in children's church just like the kids would click out in the adult service.)

SINGING

Put on a worship CD and sing to the Lord with your family. *"Speaking to one another in psalms and hymns and spiritual songs, singing, and making melody with your heart to the Lord."* Ephesians 5:19 (NAS)

INSTRUMENTS

The Bible says to praise Him on the loud cymbals. It's good to be loud when we praise God. Kids, especially pre-school children, love to play tambourines and other instruments. *"Praise Him with the sound of the trumpet, praise Him with the psaltery and harp. Praise Him with the timbrel and dance:*

praise Him with stringed instruments and organs. Praise Him upon the loud cymbals: praise Him upon the high sounding cymbals." Psalms 150:3-5

SHOUTING

Little boys love to shout. We shout at football games, so we can shout in church. The Bible tells us to "Shout unto the Lord!" *"Shout joyfully to God, all the earth; sing the glory of His name; Make His praise glorious. Say to God, How awesome are Thy works! Because of the greatness of Thy power Thine enemies will have feigned obedience to Thee."* Psalms 66:1-3 (NAS)

DANCING

A lot of men have trouble with this one, but it's not that hard, and it's really liberating. If it helps you, put on a praise tape or CD. *"You turned my wailing into dancing; you removed my sackcloth and clothed me with joy."* Psalms 30:11 (NIV)

JUMPING LEAPING AND RUNNING

Little boys love this one too. *"And he leaping up stood, and walked, and entered with them into the temple, walking, and leaping, and praising God."* Acts 3:8

LIFTING HANDS

When we lift our hands to Jesus we are surrendering our life to Him. Practice singing a song and lifting your hands.

"I will therefore that men pray every where, lifting up holy

hands, without wrath and doubting." I Timothy 2:8

KNEELING

Practice kneeling while singing a song to Jesus. *"O come, let us worship and bow down; let us kneel before the Lord our maker."* Psalms 95:6

TONGUES

The first time anybody spoke in tongues in Acts 2, they were speaking the wonderful works of God. The Holy Spirit gives us this supernatural gift to worship God. It really helps when we run out of words to describe how good God is. The more you pray in tongues around your children, the bolder they will be to pray in tongues. *"....we do hear them speak in our tongues the wonderful works of God."* Acts 2:11

BE STILL (QUIET)

We can worship God by being quiet. (Practice being quiet for 60 seconds.) *"Be still, and know that I am God; I will be exalted among the heathen, I will be exalted in the earth."* Psalms 46:10

TEARS

Sometimes we love God so much we just cry. *"When a woman who had lived a sinful life in that town learned that Jesus was eating at the Pharisee's house, she brought an alabaster jar of perfume, and as she stood behind him at his feet weeping, she began to wet his feet with her tears. Then she wiped them with her hair, kissed them and poured perfume on them."* Luke 7:37-38 (NIV)

Participation is the key to anointed praise and worship. There is an anointing when we enter into worship by singing, lifting our hands, dancing, singing in tongues, or kneeling.

Sometimes you will hear people complaining about a worship service, "Worship wasn't anointed today." Well, try singing! It's more anointed when you sing. Try dancing! It's more anointed when you dance. People sometimes have a misconception that it's up to the worship leaders to perform or bring in the anointing, but really it's up to all of us. God inhabits the praises of His people. We all need to participate—that's why we call it corporate worship.

We were created for this purpose: to worship the Lord and bring Him glory. Sometimes I wish we called ourselves "worshipers" instead of calling ourselves "Christians." It would help us to remember why we are here.

1 Paul Baloche, *Happy Song, First Love,* (Integrity Music)

CHAPTER SEVEN

Does God Speak to Kids?

*Whom shall he teach knowledge? And whom shall he
make to understand doctrine? Them that are weaned from
the milk, and drawn from the breasts. —Isaiah 28:9*

D oes God speak to kids? Emphatically, YES! God spoke to
kids and teens in the Bible and He still speaks to kids
today.

I remember when I began in full time ministry in 1979. I
had just graduated from Bible school and moved to Port
Huron, Michigan, to help my former youth pastor pioneer a
church.

We immediately began to travel and conduct kids' crusades
throughout the Midwest. This was an exciting time because at
every church we went to, most of the kids in children's church
would get saved and filled with the Holy Ghost. I'll never forget a Pentecostal church in Kentucky when 35 children were
filled with the Holy Ghost in one night. Some people said,
"Revival broke out in children's church." But really we were
just the first people to teach about the Holy Spirit and give an
altar call in children's church. Some people think it's hard to get

kids filled with the Holy Ghost but really it's easy. If you preach about it, they will believe it.

The Lord gave me a sermon in 1979 that I still preach today entitled, "The Holy Ghost will take the Chicken out of You." I talked about how Peter denied Christ three times, but then on the day of Pentecost, he stood up and boldly preached to thousands. What changed Peter? The Holy Ghost took the "chicken" out of Peter.

Then we did a puppet skit about a boy named Robby who was afraid to witness to "Bully." Along comes Sally who prays with Robby to be filled with the Holy Ghost and to receive boldness. Sally lays her hands on Robby's head, then Robby's heart (the heart puppet) would come up and speak in tongues, suddenly Robby would start speaking in tongues and lose his "chicken." Robby then proceeded to boldly witness to "Bully" and "Bully" got saved.

After writing skits about the Holy Spirit for years, we published our skits in a curriculum called the Super Church Curriculum Series. (The Super Church Curriculum Series is a three-year children's church curriculum which focuses on revival and the ministry of the Holy Spirit.) It was amazing the persecution we received when we first published Super Church. It wasn't the denominational churches that were mad; it was the Pentecostal churches. Some said we emphasized tongues too much. Some said puppets shouldn't pray in tongues. Some people even accused us of committing the unpardonable sin by blaspheming the Holy Ghost.

Of course, I wasn't mocking the Holy Ghost. My heart was to get children filled with the Holy Ghost. We've prayed with over 10,000 children to receive the Holy Spirit in 20 years of ministering to children. Today over 4,000 churches are using Super Church Curriculum worldwide. The devil really fought us in the beginning (he did not want children to be taught the Pentecostal message), but God has blessed our obedience to Him.

I had been teaching children for about two years on things like salvation, baptism in the Holy Spirit, and healing. One morning in 1981, I asked the Lord what I should teach our kids next. His response shocked me. I heard a still small voice say, "Teach them about the gifts of the Holy Spirit."

I thought, "No way! That's too deep to teach kids." I remember one time when a 12-year-old boy stood up and gave out a prophecy in one of my Kids' Crusades, and I thought, "No way! That's not God. A 12 year old can't prophesy." I wanted God to move in the service but I wanted him to move through me! (As I think back, it hurt my pride that God used a 12-year-old instead of me.) This is one of the main stumbling blocks for children. Adults don't want kids to step out into these things because it hurts our pride and we want to be in control.

I have found out in my walk with God that He delights in hurting our pride, because He wants us humble. (God never dishonors us because we are valuable to Him, but He does want us to let go of our pride.) This is another thing we can learn from children—humility.

MATTHEW 18:3-4 (AMP)

3 And said, Truly I say to you, unless you repent (change, turn about) and become like little children [trusting, lowly, loving, forgiving], you can never enter the kingdom of heaven [at all].

4 Whoever will humble himself therefore and become like this little child [trusting, lowly, loving, forgiving] is greatest in the kingdom of heaven.

I began to pray and ask God, "How do I teach children about the gifts of the Spirit?" I don't know anybody that I could call and ask this question. There wasn't any curriculum or books written on teaching kids about the gifts, so I just prayed.

There were several things the Lord showed me:

Number one: Worship was key, because God inhabits the praises of His people, so I spent a month or two teaching on praise and worship. I won't go into details here because I covered worship in the last chapter.

Number two: If children were going to be able to prophesy and step out in the gifts of the Spirit they would have to know how to hear God's voice. So I spent about a month teaching kids how to hear God's voice.

Number three: Use familiar Bible stories to teach kids about the gifts. For example, when God spoke to Noah and told him the flood was coming, that was the gift of prophecy and a word of wisdom combined. The word of wisdom deals with God's plan in the future. When telling the Bible story of Noah, talk about how God gave Noah a word of wisdom. A good teacher goes from the known to the unknown.

Number four: Don't be afraid to use visuals, puppets, or drama to convey the written Word. I wrote puppet skits and drama skits where God spoke to Robby, Sally, and Joey, and this would cause faith to rise in the hearts of the children. (Kids will naturally imitate what they see the puppets do. They think, "Hey, if God can speak to Robby, He can speak to me.")

THREE PARTS OF MAN

I knew that before I could teach children on "How to hear the voice of God" I needed to teach on the three-fold nature of man.

I THESSALONIANS 5:23

....I pray God your whole spirit and soul and body be preserved blameless unto the coming of our Lord Jesus Christ.

We have three parts: spirit, soul and body. I like to put it this way: I am a spirit. I have a soul. I live in a body.

It's important to drive home the point that God speaks to us through our spirit. If I stand up in front of a group of children and say, "God spoke to me," they are going to think that I heard an audible voice. (Sometimes God does speak in an audible voice, but most of the time He talks to your spirit – inside of you, with a still, small voice.)

I find there are four primary ways that God speaks to us through our spirit:

Number One: The Inward Witness

The primary (most frequent) way that God leads all of His children is by the inward witness.

ROMANS 8:16

The Spirit of God bears witness with our spirit that we are the children of God.

With the inward witness, you don't hear anything. It is a "spiritual feeling" that you have in your gut. It's a red light or green light. You may be watching a TV show and you get a yucky feeling on the inside. That's the red light, the inward witness, telling you to turn off the tube.

Sometimes you'll hear people say, "I've got peace about that." What they are saying is, "I have a green light; the inward witness is telling me to go for it."

Spiritual Exercise

I was praying for a tangible way to communicate what the inward witness was to my kids, when the Lord gave me an idea. I call it a spiritual exercise.

First, I led all the children in a worship song. Then we worshiped in tongues for a few minutes. Next I asked all the kids to bow their heads, close their eyes, and just be still and listen. I then proceeded to make positive statements that agreed with God's Word like, "Jesus is your healer." And statements that disagrees with God's Word like, "God put this sickness on you to teach you a lesson."

Then I asked the children, "What did it feel like inside when I said, "Jesus is your healer?"

"A good feeling," they responded.

"And what kind of a feeling did you get when I said, 'God put this sickness on you to teach you a lesson.'"

"A yucky feeling."

I tell the children, "See, that's the inward witness. It's on a small scale, but it is the same inward witness that will help you on decisions like, who to be friends with, who to marry, what you're going to do when you grow up." The inward witness is not as spectacular as a dream or a vision, but it is supernatural.

Number Two: The Voice of Your Spirit (Your Conscience)

The second most frequent way that God speaks to us is by

the voice of our own spirit, which is our conscience.

ACTS 23:1
And Paul earnestly, beholding the council, said, Men and brethren, I have lived in all good conscience before God until this day.

Your conscience is a still, small voice, the voice of your spirit.

I KINGS 19:12
And after the earthquake a fire; but the Lord was not in the fire: and after the fire a still small voice.

If you have been born again, your conscience is a safe guide. If you're not born again, your conscience is not a safe guide. The inward voice is a little different than the inward witness in that you actually hear words on the inside of you—a still small voice.

One way I taught kids about listening to the voice of their spirit was to put them in real life situations. "How many of you have ever been tempted to steal a candy bar at a grocery store, but you heard a voice say, 'No'?" "How many of you have ever walked past your bedroom, and seeing it all messy, you heard a voice say, 'Remember, Mom told you to clean up your room'?" That is your conscience—the voice of your spirit—sometimes called the inward voice.

Spiritual Exercise

I also did a spiritual exercise with children to teach them about the inward voice. I would have everyone worship for about five minutes. Then I asked everyone to bow their heads and close their eyes. "Listen to your heart," I would say. We would wait about 60 seconds just listening to our hearts. "Did anybody hear anything?" Many children would raise their hand. I asked them one at a time to come forward and tell us (with the microphone) what they heard. (This helps to get the children confident enough to stand up and give out a word or a prophecy if the Holy Spirit gives them one.)

The children would say things like:

"Jesus loves me."

"He told me to tell my friends about Him."

"He told me to be nice to my sister."

Then I would say something to the kids like this:

"See, that is the voice of your spirit, your conscience talking to you. Your body has a voice. It tells you when it's hungry. Your mind has a voice, the voice of reason. Your spirit has a voice too, your conscience." (Mom and Dad, you can do this same exercise at home during devotions.)

What you heard today was your spirit talking to you. Sometimes you will hear words that Jesus wants you to share with everyone. That's what we call a prophecy. If the Holy Spirit gives you a prophecy then He will also anoint you to share it with others.

Most people who miss it with prophecy do so because they try to prophesy something that was just for them. (For example, you would never stand up and give out a prophecy like, "Thus saith the Lord, clean your room." That was just for you.)

LEARNING TO LISTEN

Mom and Dad, it is very important that your children learn how to listen to their conscience and obey God in the small things.

I TIMOTHY 4:1-2

1 Now the Spirit speaketh expressly, that in the latter times some shall depart from the faith, giving heed to seducing spirits, and doctrines of devils;

2 Speaking lies in hypocrisy; having the conscience seared with a hot iron;

It's hard to believe but these verses are talking about people who once were believers, but now they've "departed from the faith" because their conscience became seared. If you disobey your conscience repeatedly, eventually your conscience will become seared. This is not a good place to be because it's a place where you can't hear God. This is a place where you don't know right from wrong. I've met "Christians" who have no problem lying; in fact they believe their own lies. This is what happens when your conscience becomes seared. Proverbs

20:27 says, *"....the spirit of man is the candle of the Lord."* When your conscience becomes seared, the light goes out.

I was children's pastor at Life of Faith Fellowship in Port Huron, Michigan, in 1979. One couple at the church had two daughters, Stacy, who was six, and Debbie, who was four. One day, Debbie asked her mom if she could spend the night at a friend's house who lived next door.

Debbie's mom didn't know how to respond because their neighbors weren't Christians, however, she didn't want to say anything negative about the neighbors. She responded by saying, "Mommy needs to pray about that," hoping that Debbie would just forget.

Ten minutes later, Debbie came back, "Mom, did you pray about that yet?"

"No, dear, I haven't. Ask me later."

Ten minutes later, Deb appeared again, "Mom, did you pray about it yet?"

This happened several times before her Mom responded, "Debbie, why don't you pray about it? You go sit in the green chair in the living room, pray in tongues, listen to your heart, and tell me what your heart says."

When her mom came walking through the living room, sure enough, Debbie was sitting in the green chair praying in tongues. Five minutes later, Deb approached her mom. "Mom, my heart told me not to spend the night at the neighbor's house."

Praise the Lord! Debbie had learned how to listen to her heart at four years old. It's good for children to obey their parents, but it's better if they learn how to hear God's voice and obey God on their own. Mom and Dad won't always be around, especially when they grow up and one of their friends says to them, "How would you like to try one of these little, green pills?"

Sometimes Christian kids grow up and never disobey their parents, but then backslide when they get to college because they don't know how to make decisions. Mom and Dad always told them what to do, and they don't know how to hear from God for themselves.

You still hold veto power, Mom and Dad, but begin to let your children make some decisions on their own. Teach them how to pray about things and listen to their heart.

NUMBER THREE: THE VOICE OF THE SPIRIT OF GOD

Another way that God speaks to us is through the voice of the Spirit of God. This voice is an inner voice, but it is much stronger and more authoritative than the voice of your spirit.

ROMANS 8:14

For as many as are led by the Spirit of God, they are the sons of God.

When God spoke to the child Samuel, I do not believe that

it was an audible voice. If it were an audible voice, Eli would have heard it too. The voice was so strong inside Samuel that it seemed audible to him. This is the voice of the Spirit of God. You will hear this voice much less frequently than the voice of your own spirit.

NUMBER FOUR: VISIONS (SEEING AND KNOWING)

Another way that God speaks to us is through pictures or visions. Many times God will show us a picture of something. This is not you trying to think up something in your imagination, but the Holy Ghost showing you a picture in your spirit.

For example, one time I was praying for a lady at a church in London, England. While I was praying for her, I had my eyes closed, but I saw a picture of my mother. I thought that was odd, but then I asked this question:

"Are you in fellowship with your mom?"

"Oh no," she said "I haven't talked to her in years. I did just get a letter from her, but I don't really want to respond."

I told her what I saw and then added, "I believe that God wants you to restore your relationship with your mom."

Another time, I was in children's church at Living Word Christian Center when I was associate pastor. It was during the worship part of the service and I saw a picture of a bicycle in my spirit.

I wasn't sure what that meant so I asked, "Is anybody here praying for a bicycle?"

About ten children responded, so I screened each one of them and I narrowed it down to one child who had been praying for a bicycle for some time. Once I found the boy, I felt a little funny because I didn't have a bicycle to give him so I just encouraged him to keep believing in God.

The next day, we received a phone call at the church office about the bicycle. There was a little boy in the class who had bought a new bike about two weeks earlier, and then he had just won a new bike in a sweepstakes. He wanted to give the sweepstakes bike to the boy who had been praying for a bike. Praise God! I didn't know that the boy with the two bikes was in Super Church that day, but the Holy Ghost did!

GIFTS OF THE SPIRIT

After teaching your children about how to hear the voice of God, you will want to teach them about the gifts of the Spirit. We find the gifts of the Spirit listed in I Corinthians, chapter twelve.

I CORINTHIANS 12:1
Now concerning spiritual gifts, brethren, I would not have you ignorant.

God doesn't want us ignorant about spiritual gifts and He doesn't want our children ignorant either.

It's important we establish that "spiritual gifts" are supernatural; they are not natural gifts. These are gifts from the Holy Spirit, so they must be supernatural. For example, when the Bible talks about "gifts of healings," it's not talking about doctors. It's talking about supernatural healing. It's interesting to note that the Bible isn't against doctors (Luke was a physician), but it only testifies about supernatural healings, the kind that brings glory to God.

I CORINTHIANS 12:7-11

7 But the manifestation of the Spirit is given to every man of profit withal.

8 For to one is given by the Spirit the word of wisdom; to another the word of knowledge by the same Spirit;

9 To another faith by the same Spirit; to another the gifts of healing by the same Spirit;

10 To another the working of miracles; to another prophecy; to another discerning of spirits; to another divers kinds of tongues; to another the interpretation of tongues:

11 But all these worketh that one and the selfsame Spirit, dividing to every man severally as he will."

There are nine gifts of the Spirit and they can by divided into three categories:

Gifts of Inspiration—Gifts That Say Something
• Gift of tongues—speaking in a unknown language

- Interpretation of tongues—interpreting what is spoken in an unknown language
- Prophecy—God speaks to His body for the purpose of edification, exhortation, or comfort

Gifts of Revelation—Gifts That Reveal Something

- Word of wisdom—Reveals the future
- Word of knowledge—Supernatural knowledge about the present and the past
- Discerning of spirits—Seeing into the spirit world, such as angels or demons

Gifts of Power —Gifts That Do Something

- Gift of faith—Supernatural faith (beyond ordinary faith) that comes on you to do something like raising the dead
- Working of miracles—works a miracle like turning water into wine
- Gifts of healings—Supernatural healing of disease or sickness

I would encourage you to get a good book and study in the gifts of the Spirit. Howard Carter, Gordon Lindsay, Lester Sumrall, and Kenneth Hagin have all written good books on the gifts of the Spirit.

Once you understand them, begin to teach your children about the gifts. Instill faith in your kids by telling them that God wants to use them in the gifts. The Bible says in Acts 2:17,

"And it shall come to pass in the last days, saith God, I will pour out of my Spirit upon all flesh: and your sons and your daughter shall prophesy."

CHAPTER EIGHT

Let The Children Lead

"....a little child shall lead them."   — Isaiah 11:6

It's easy for a parent or a teacher to recognize leadership gifts in their children. If I can spend several hours teaching and observing a group of children, I can pick out who the leaders are. One thing about people who have leadership gifts is that they will find a way to use their gifts. It is much better if I have the peer leaders on my side, leading the children in a godly direction, than for the peer leaders to be pulling against me. If I don't find a place for children to use their leadership, then they will end up pulling against me.

The same is true for the local church. If young people and children feel that the church has no place for them to use their leadership gifts, then one of two things will happen. Number one, they will leave the church, or number two, they will stay, but use their gifts to pull against the leadership and cause division.

In twenty years of ministering to children, I did have to ask one child to leave Super Church and not come back until he had repented and changed. This was a twelve-year-old boy who was constantly challenging my authority and using his leadership in a negative way. In every other case, I have succeeded in getting the peer leaders to be on my side. One way I do this is by getting them involved in ministry.

From 1983-1986 I was Children's Pastor at Family Worship Center in Tulsa, Oklahoma. Tulsa was an interesting city because there were so many Bible students in town. These were quality people with a zeal for the things of God and some of them would get involved in children's ministry.

Every September, we would get many new recruits, but in May, there was always a great exodus. One year I lost half of my work force in May.

In the summer of 1985, I was complaining to the Lord because by the time I would get people trained they would leave. I told the Lord, "It takes me six months to get people trained in puppetry. We had quality puppetry for three months of the year, and then they leave."

The Holy Ghost whispered back to me, "Use the kids."

"That's not going to work, God. They are not old enough," I responded.

"Use the kids," I heard again.

"They don't have the arm strength," I argued.

"Use the kids. They've been sitting under your ministry for three years and they are committed to you."

"Okay, God," I said, "I'll use the kids. I know this won't work, but just to prove to You that You're wrong, I'll use the kids." (Now, don't tell me you have never thought that about something God has said to you.)

So, I obeyed God and prayerfully selected seven children from Super Church to be part of the Super Church Puppet Team. In two short months we had some great puppeteers. They learned quicker than the adults did.

As I got into this, I began to see it was an incredible opportunity for discipleship and leadership training. Before 1985, all I was doing was preaching and teaching kids; I really wasn't pastoring kids. In 1985, I took my first step toward pastoring and discipling children by starting the puppet team. I always told the kids that I was not training them for puppets; I was training them for ministry.

LEAD BY A TWELVE-YEAR-OLD

In June of 1986 I witnessed one the of the most powerful revival services I have ever been a part of. I was still Children's Pastor at Family Worship Center. I had asked a friend of mine, Bill Bush, to be the speaker at our summer kid's camp.

The first night of camp did not go very well. For some reason Bill was really struggling. I just thought in my mind, "Oh, well, tomorrow night will go better."

The second night of camp, I introduced Bill following praise and worship. Bill didn't do a puppet skit, drama skit or anything like that. He just stood up at the front of the chapel with a rock in his hand.

"Boys and girls," Bill said. "I was driving to camp tonight and the Lord spoke to me to stop my van and pick up this rock that was on the side of the road. He told me to tell you that some of you here are like this rock. You have a hard heart."

At this point I wondered where Bill was going with this.

"Some people don't think you can have a hard heart unless you're lost, but you can harden your heart toward God just like you can harden your heart toward a friend. Has a friend ever said something that hurt you so much that you didn't want to be their friend anymore? What did you do? You hardened your heart toward your friend.

"How do you know if you have hardened your heart toward God? Do you have a hard time going to church? Do you have a hard time lifting your hands or dancing during worship? Do you have a hard time witnessing to your friends about Jesus? What would you think of a friend who only wanted to be your friend when others weren't around? He wouldn't be much of a friend would he? Yet, that is how many of us treat the Lord."

Bill went on to say, "If that is you, if you've hardened your heart toward God, then I want you to come down to the front, repent and ask God to forgive you for having a hard heart."

For about five or ten seconds nothing happened. It was very quiet. You could hear a pin drop.

I thought to myself, "Maybe Bill missed it. That was kind of a hard word. If this doesn't work, the service is over." (I could tell that Bill didn't have anything planned other than this "rock.")

Chris was a 12-year-old boy who was the class clown. He was on the ministry team and helped me with puppets, but he was never serious about anything. Chris would crack jokes while I was preaching. Many times I wanted to laugh at his jokes, but knew I couldn't. I had jokingly said I didn't know whether to hug Chris or to slap him!

Chris was also a church kid. He was the music minister's son and had grown up in church. He never took God or church very seriously, but he was well-liked and popular. Chris was definitely one of the peer leaders in children's church—that is why I asked him to be on the ministry team. I wanted him pulling with me, not away from me.

After about 5 or 10 seconds of quiet (which seemed like an eternity), Chris suddenly stood up from the back row and ran down to the altar. When Chris ran to the altar something swept into the room—the presence of the Holy Spirit. A spirit of prayer and repentance fell on the chapel. Everyone, adults and children alike, began to weep and most of us ran to the altar to repent for having a hard heart. My kids, ages 6-12 years old, spent an hour up at the altar repenting, weeping, and praying.

This was one of the most powerful services I have ever been in. We were led into that revival by a 12-year-old boy.

DON'T LAY ASIDE THE SUPERNATURAL

That night changed my life. I went back to my pew and sat down, and I heard the voice of God saying to me, "Your work

32000

here is done. It's time for you to go." I wasn't thinking about leaving, having been at Family Worship Center for three years, but I saw I had layed aside the supernatural side of my ministry.

When we got back home, I was trying to tell the parents what God had done at camp, but they didn't understand. "What? Kids were crying and repenting?" They just looked at me like a cow at a new gate.

It was during that camp that Bill told me about a church in Minneapolis, Minnesota, that was looking for a children's pastor. Pastor Mac Hammond had called Bill and offered him the job, but Bill wasn't interested. I had been at Pastor Mac's church in 1985 to minister at a camp meeting, so I knew about the church and knew Pastor Mac.

I remember saying to Bill, "That is a good church. Someone ought to take the job. If I wasn't so happy here, I'd take it." (I did not want to leave where I was.)

It took a couple of months for God to get it across to me that He wanted me to go work with Pastor Mac. Being at Living Word was a real stretch for me. The church had about 1,200 members and we had about 250-300 kids in Super Church. I had to learn how to develop leaders and how to delegate.

Another reason God sent Debbie and me to Living Word was to learn how to pray and intercede. Now, I had read many books on prayer and taught prayer, but there was more I needed to learn.

I really didn't know very much about intercession or soul

travail. Prayer was the heart of the church at Living Word. Lynne Hammond was in charge of the prayer ministry and had spent many years praying by herself, then training others to pray.

I never forgot my first kids' camp at Living Word. It was August of 1987. Camp started on Monday night with an evening service. (Bill was our guest speaker again.) The service was great, but I knew we were just warming up.

Tuesday morning, after breakfast, we met in the chapel for "morning prayer." I just planned on making a few announcements and then to pray for about ten minutes. To my surprise, three or four girls came to the front and began to pray, intercede, and weep. I had never seen anything like this, especially with kids. I didn't know what to do. I knew that the girls' moms were all involved in the prayer ministry and in fact, one of the girls was Mac and Lynne's daughter, Lucy. I didn't feel like I should stop the girls from praying, and yet we had a schedule to keep.

Finally I said, "If you want to stay and pray you can or you can go to camp activities."

To my surprise about six or seven girls stayed to pray. I could tell that they knew more about prayer than I did, so I just sat down and watched them. They prayed for about one hour.

That night at the camp service we had an awesome time. While Bill was praying for kids, I felt a spirit of prophecy come on me. Bill must have sensed it too because he looked at me and said, "Do you have anything?"

I stood up and began to prophesy over the children. I had a word for every child that I prayed for. It was powerful. It seemed to me that I could have prophesied over everyone in the building. That had never happened to me before or since. After the service I was thinking about it and I thought, "Wow, I wonder where that came from?"

The Spirit of God spoke to me, "Do you remember the girls who were praying this morning? That is where this came from. They prayed it in."

Wow! I'm so glad I didn't stop them from praying, even if I didn't understand it.

When I came on staff at Living Word, one of the first things I did was start a puppet team like I had in Tulsa. I taught a class on puppets for four weeks and then selected kids, teens, and adults from that class to be a part of the puppet team.

I was seeking God about direction for my ministry during a staff prayer advance in 1988. Our church staff would take one day a month to pray all day at a cabin in the woods. It was during this prayer time that I had a vision of the future. I saw myself standing in the balcony above Super Church. Super Church was full with about 250 kids. There was a lot of activity going on, but I noticed that about 90% of the ministry was being done by children.

I saw children leading praise and worship. I saw kids ushering and greeting new kids. I saw children praying at the altar with other children for salvation and the infilling of the Holy Spirit. I saw children doing puppets and drama and even the sound.

The Spirit of God spoke to me and said, "I want you to train children in these other ministries just like you have trained the puppet team kids."

I responded, "Lord, I don't have time to train all these kids in all of these ministries."

He assured me that He would send me leaders to help train them for these other ministries.

Peggy Johnson was our first leader. She was involved in the evangelism ministry at Living Word. Pastor Nick Kinn was on staff as a full time street evangelist. Nick would take people out on the street several times a week to pass out tracts and witness. I've never seen anyone who has a gift for personal evangelism like Nick.

One day Peggy took her eight-year-old son, Robby, and some of his friend to the park to play. There was a jungle gym in the shape of a boat that the kids were playing on. They began to pretend that the boat was Noah's ark and started putting the imaginary animals on the ark and prepare for the flood. As they were busy preparing, Robby spoke up, "Hey, before the flood comes we need to witness."

This group of children looked around for someone to witness to. There was a little boy riding his bicycle through the park on the bike path. These four or five children went and surrounded the boy on his bike.

"Do you know Jesus?" they asked.

"No, I'm Jewish," the boy responded.

"That's okay, you can still know Jesus," Robby added.

Basically, they wouldn't let this kid leave until he prayed with them. Peggy was watching all this happen with tears streaming down her face. The Holy Ghost spoke to Peggy that day. He told her to train these children to be witnesses for the Lord. (Notice how God used Robby to minister to his mom.)

Peggy approached me in the lobby of the church and said she wanted to take kids out on the streets to witness. Tears were streaming down her face as she recounted the story. It bore witness with the vision I had seen just two weeks earlier.

I said to her, "Peggy, I don't know how to do what you're talking about. I don't know anyone else who is doing this. I don't know anyone you could call to ask how, but I know this is God, so go for it."

Peggy didn't need much motivation. In a short time, she had trained 25 kids to evangelize. We called the ministry "CIA" meaning Children In Action. Peggy trained the children like Pastor Nick trained the adults. In the first year of witnessing they prayed with over 1,000 children to be born again. (The kids prayed with more children to get saved that year than the children's ministry staff did.)

One day I was praying and the Lord said to me that I had a "John the Baptist Ministry." I would prepare the way for people that would do a greater work than I did. After our ministry team trip this past summer (1998) at Joy Christian Center, I asked some of the children to testify about the trip. One boy, Cory, who was 12 years old, testified that he saw a vision of himself as a children's pastor, but he had the same hair cut he has now (a bowl cut.) He saw himself preaching to hundreds of kids. Then he added that he was a lot better than Pastor Mark. (My response to him was that he had better be better than me—a lot better.)

Shortly after Peggy talked with me, Jill Almquist approached me. Jill was a part of Lynne's prayer ministry. Jill had it on her heart to teach children to pray and intercede. We began a prayer ministry for children which met on Wednesday nights. Again, we had never heard about anyone else doing this. Jill was led by the Spirit in how to lead them. Ten years later, Jill, is still leading the children's prayer group on Wednesday nights at Living Word.

I then talked to Jerre Sibinski about training children to lead praise and worship in Super Church. We eventually had a full band and a team of young praise and worship leaders.

We ended up with six ministries that were designed to disciple children and use their leadership gifts.

- Prayer Ministry (Intercession for souls)
- Children In Action (Evangelism)
- Usher Ministry

- Puppet Team Ministry
- Audio/Visual Ministry
- Praise and Worship Ministry

Today ten of the children who were on our puppet team, are now grown-up and on staff, full-time, at Living Word Christian Center. One young man who was involved with the A.V. ministry is now part of the television ministry. One girl who was involved with the puppet team is now the junior high pastor with her husband. There are two girls who are grade school teachers at Maranatha Christian Academy, a Christian school in Minnepolis.

I think that most churches in America do a good job of teaching kids, but it stops right there. I also think that most churches in America do a poor job of discipling children and youth. There is rarely any focus whatsoever on developing their leadership gifts and abilities so they can be used in God's kingdom.

I read in a youth ministry article that 80% of teens don't feel that their church needs them. They feel if they left their church they wouldn't be missed. This has got to change. If we would take some time and disciple our young people and develop their leadership gifts they wouldn't feel this way. The youth and children are the greatest untapped resource in our churches today. They are literally a sleeping giant.

MATTHEW 28:19 (NIV)

Therefore go and make disciples of all nations, baptizing them in the name of the Father and the Son and of the Holy Spirit.

Jesus told us to make disciples of all nations. The word "disciple" means, a taught or trained one. In the local church we not only need to teach—we also need to train our children and youth for ministry, prayer and evangelism.

I looked up the word "pastor" in W.E. Vines Greek dictionary. It stated, "a shepherd, one who tends, herds or flocks, not merely one who feeds them."

Pastoring involves more than simply feeding—it also involves discipleship and training. Jesus taught the multitudes, but He pastored the twelve disciples. What was different in His relationship with the disciples and His relationship with the multitudes? He gave the disciples something to do. He got them involved in His ministry. Jesus spent more quality time with His disciples where He poured out His heart to them.

MATTHEW 9:36-38

36 But when he saw the multitudes, he was moved with compassion on them, because they fainted, and were scattered abroad, as sheep having no shepherd.

37 Then saith he unto his disciples, The harvest truly is plenteous, but the laborers are few;

38 Pray ye therefore the Lord of the harvest, that he will send forth laborers into his harvest.

When Jesus called the twelve disciples, I imagine that some thought He was forming a little clique. But His heart was to reach the harvest. "The harvest is plenteous, but the laborers are few."

Immediately following Matthew 9:38 we find Matthew 10:1

MATTHEW 10:1, 5-8

1 And when he called unto him his twelve disciples, he gave them power against unclean spirits, to cast them out, and to heal all manner of sickness and all manner of disease.

5 These twelve Jesus sent forth, and commanded them, saying, go not into the way of the Gentiles...

6 But go rather to the lost sheep of the house of Israel.

7 And as you go, preach, saying, the kingdom of heaven is at hand.

8 Heal the sick, cleanse the lepers, raise the dead, cast out devils: freely you have received, freely give.

We need to do the same thing with our children and our youth that Jesus did with His disciples. We need to give them opportunities to minister and be involved in what we are doing. This is also an area you need to explore if you are involved in full time ministry. Debra and I have always involved

Mark, Jr., and Melissa, in whatever we are doing for God. (We wouldn't lose so many "preachers kids" if more ministers would do this.)

A Fresh Vision

My vision for revival is to lead children and youth into revival and then get out of the way. In the summer of 1997, I was speaking at a kids camp near Fergus Falls, Minnesota. This was the same group of children from Community Bible Church that I mentioned in the introduction. Pastor Greg Permann had invited me back to speak.

I was excited because God had moved in a powerful way the year before. On Tuesday night at camp I preached a message on "He's a Father to the Fatherless." I then asked all the kids who did not have a father living at home with them to come forward for prayer. (This is something the Lord has instructed me do everywhere I go.)

Pastor Greg and I prayed for the Father to touch these children in a powerful way and to let them experience the length and breadth and depth and height of His love.

After praying for "the fatherless," I made a general call like this, "If anyone is hungry for more of God and you want prayer, then come forward."

Almost everyone in the room stood up. There were too many for Pastor Greg and me to pray for by ourselves so I asked some of the worship band and teenage counselors to help pray.

I didn't know it, but most of the youth group had been to the revival at Brownsville Assembly of God that summer and there was a powerful anointing on them as they began to pray.

At about 10:00 p.m. (service had been going since 7:00 p.m.) I noticed that some of the kids were not entering in any more so I made an announcement that if they wanted to go to the campfire they could, or if they wanted, they could stay and pray.

At that point Pastor Greg and I just sat down and watched the Holy Spirit do His thing. (This is what I mean when I say my goal is to lead children into revival and then get out of the way.)

There were children praying for other children and teenagers praying for children. Kids were laying all over the floor under the power of the Holy Spirit. Some kids were shaking, some were laughing, some were crying. At about 11:00 p.m., some of the kids from the campfire came back and said, "Hey, is the service still going on?"

They decided to come in and get prayed for again. That service lasted past midnight. Wow! I've never been in a five-hour kids' service where the children were there by their own free will.

It's time to let our children and our young people lead.

CHAPTER NINE

A Fresh Wind Of Revival

After seeing how fired up and powerful the teenagers were in Fergus Falls, I had a desire to go to Brownsville and see what God was doing there.

In May of 1998, Deb, myself, and our children made the trip to Pensacola, Florida. All I can say about Brownsville is that it was powerful. Several things impressed me about the revival at Brownsville.

One was that they seemed to be strong in every area that I feel is really important:

- The praise and worship was awesome
- There was a strong emphasis on winning the lost
- The youth ministry was strong
- The children's ministry was strong
- Prayer was intertwined with every fabric of the church
- There was a model of a pastor and evangelist working together, both secure in their callings and giftings

It was great to see a church hitting on all eight cylinders. At the Friday night baptism service, I just sat and wept as new converts shared their testimonies and were baptized in water. Surely this is what a water baptism was meant to be.

The thing that impressed me the most at Brownsville, though, was how they included the youth and the children in the revival. The youth and children have their own services once a week, but they were also a part of the revival services each evening. I believe that Brownsville is a forerunner of what is going to happen in the coming revival.

The week we were in Brownsville was the same week that a teenager shot 22 people at his high school in Washington state. On Saturday night, the youth were seated in the choir seats helping to lead the praise and worship. When Pastor Kilpatrick took the pulpit, he said, "I think tonight is the night that we need to pray for our schools."

In a matter of seconds after he said that, most of the youth were on their knees in deep travail. A spirit of prayer fell on the congregation as we began to pray and intercede for our schools. To be honest, I've never seen youth like the youth I saw at Brownsville.

Why are the youth so powerful in Brownsville? I'm sure there are many reasons, but one, I believe, is because they have been given a place for ministry and are included in the revival. Charity Jones who sings the song, "Mercy Seat" for the altar call, at most of the revival services, was 14 years old when the revival began over three years ago.

Think about it. What a testimony!

"What did you do in high school?"

"I sang for the altar call at the Brownsville Revival every

night and watched 150,000 people get saved."

I know this is what I want for my kids. My son is 12 and my daughter is 10 right now. If I didn't know I was called to be in Minnesota, I'd pack my bags and move to Brownsville just so my kids could grow up in that church. However, God doesn't want us to all pack our bags and move to Brownsville. He wants us to take revival to our cities and our nation.

In August of 1998, we took our children from Joy Christian Center to a kids' camp at Big Sandy Camp. We were joining with kids from Living Word Christian Center. John Tasch was the camp speaker. On the last night of camp, we were praying around the altar. I was praying and interceding for the fatherless children in our nation. I had my eyes closed, but I saw a vision. In this vision I saw a school hallway. The hallway was packed with children between 10 and 14 years of age. They were busy at their lockers and walking to their next class. Then I saw a wind blow through the hallway and many of the young people were sucked into the wind. Teachers were observing this mass confusion but were powerless to stop the wind. The Spirit of God spoke to me and said, "The next revival is going to happen in our schools." The enemy thinks he has God locked out of the schools, but he is not more powerful than the power of the Holy Ghost.

Our children are the open door for us to get the Gospel into schools and reach the millions of children in America who have never heard the Gospel. You and I cannot go into schools and preach the Gospel, but children can. We need to equip them.

In the months following this vision, as Debra and I prayed about it, we began to see that the vision was a prophetic vision for our ministry. The time has come for us to step out in faith and fulfill our vision. We resigned our position as associate pastor at Joy Christian Center to focus full time on Leading Families Into Revival.

I have been involved in revival since 1995, and since that time I have spent a lot of time reading and studying about the history of revival. I noticed a pattern. Before every major revival two things happened. One was that God's people were hungry and praying for revival. Secondly, every revival had been prophesied about before it happened. The purpose of the prophecy many times was to stir God's people up to pray.

Some prophecies we just have a "wait and see if it happens" attitude, but for many prophecies the Holy Ghost is giving us direction. When God spoke to Noah about the coming flood and gave him instructions to build the ark, Noah had to do something to obey that word.

In Exodus, chapter three, verse nine, we read where God spoke to Moses through the burning bush.

EXODUS 3:9-12 (NIV)
9 "And now the cry of the Israelites has reached me, and I have seen the way the Egyptians are oppressing them.

10 So now, go. I am sending you to Pharaoh to bring my people the Israelites out of Egypt."

11 But Moses said to God, "Who am I, that I should go to Pharaoh and bring the Israelites out of Egypt?"

12 And God said, "I will be with you. And this will be the sign to you that it is I who have sent you: When you have brought the people out of Egypt, you will worship God on this mountain."

God gave Moses a sign that Moses had to fulfill. "This will be the sign that I am speaking, go and bring the children of Israel to this mountain to worship." In other words Moses had to fulfill his own prophecy. Moses had to do something to obey God.

We could just sit back and say, "Well, let's see if revival happens in our schools." Or we could take a more aggressive approach.

I can promise you this: the humanists, atheists and gay rights people are very aggressive in our schools. Just the other day, I pulled an article off the internet about a video being produced called, "It's Elementary," designed to teach elementary children about homosexuals and lesbians. It is in the public schools right now.

The following is an excerpt from that article:

The narrator's voice calmly introduces the video while the camera pans over a playground full of children playing peacefully together at a public school. "Most adults probably don't see why schools should teach young children about gay people," the voice says.

While that is no doubt true, it becomes clear in "It's Elementary" that homosexual activists see why schools should teach about the gay lifestyle. It is to capture the hearts and minds of the next generation. In fact, in an interview about the video with a Santa Fe newspaper, Chasnoff states candidly, "What's clear in the film is that the younger the kids, the more open they were.... If we could start doing this kind of education in kindergarten, first grade, second grade, we'd have a better generation." [1]

When I read this it made me mad! That's my message! Get the Gospel to the children while they are young—not just my children, but the children of the world, the children who are lost, the children who are growing up today without fathers, the children who have parents, but who are too busy making money or careers to really care for their children. I want to reach them. I think most Christians tend to take a defensive posture when we hear stuff like this, but what if we took a more aggressive approach?

WHAT IF?

I've always been a strong believer in Christian education, and we have always sent our children to Christian school. However one thing that has always bothered me is that some of the most on fire Christian kids either go to private Christian schools or they are home schooled. Many of our most committed Christian educators are teaching in private Christian schools—many times for much less money than they could make in a public school.

What if we, the body of Christ, planned a major evangelistic assault on the public schools? What if we took one year off from sending our kids to Christian schools and home schooling them? What would happen if, one year, every Christian boy and girl went to public school? Of course, the public schools would need to hire new teachers because of the increased enrollment, so the Christian educators could get the jobs at the public schools.

Our goal would be to evangelize and bring revival to the schools in America. Can you see it? I can see it. Pray about it.

If we send our children to be young evangelists in the pubic schools we would need to do three things:

NUMBER ONE

Pray for our children and youth. They will need to have the prayer backing of both home and church. In Matthew 9:38, Jesus commands us, *"Pray ye therefore the Lord of the harvest, that He will send forth laborers into His harvest."* What are we to pray for? The laborers. There is a harvest of souls in our public schools that have never heard the Gospel. We need to pray for the laborers to bring in His harvest. Who are the laborers? Our children. They are the ones who can legally preach and evangelize our schools.

Many people in America, especially children, have never heard the Gospel presented to them. I grew up in America and went to church every Sunday, but I never heard the Gospel of Jesus Christ preached until I was 16 years old.

I did a missions trip to Russia and Belarus in 1994, a few years after "the wall" fell. We did some street ministry and also went to an orphanage. I thought there would be a lot of resistance when I began to preach. But instead of resistance I sensed a pull on my gift.

At the orphanage, there were 85 children. When I gave the altar call 84 hands went up immediately. It was the most powerful evangelistic anointing I have ever experienced.

I asked Pastor Nikki, our host on this mission trip, if these kids had ever heard the Gospel before. He said, "No! It was their first time."

I thought about the harvest of children in Russia. Up until now it has been illegal to preach the Gospel of Jesus Christ to children. Older people could go to church, but children could not.

Wow! What a harvest of millions and millions of children in Russia.

I believe we have a similar situation in the pubic schools in America. Think about the harvest, the precious fruit of the earth. Millions of American children have never heard the Gospel of Jesus Christ.

We should pray for the harvest and pray over the laborers, our children. We need to pray for our children at church and at home on a regular basis. Pray for their protection. Plead the blood of Jesus over them. Pray for boldness, wisdom, and direction.

NUMBER TWO

We need to train our children to pray and intercede for the lost. I believe we cannot have effective evangelism—new births—without intercession for the lost.

John Wesley said, "It seems God is limited by our prayer life, that He can do nothing for humanity unless someone asks Him to."

MATTHEW 9:38
Pray ye therefore the Lord of the harvest, that he will send forth labourers into his harvest.

Think about this. It is HIS harvest, but He still told us to pray.

MATTHEW 6:8
....your Father knoweth what things ye have need of, before you ask Him.

He knows what we need, but He still told us to ask.

MATTHEW 18:18

....*Whatsoever ye shall bind earth shall be bound in heaven: and whatsoever ye shall loose on earth shall be loosed in heaven.*

Notice how it starts out on earth. We need to learn to intercede and travail for the lost. One way that we capture God's heart for the lost is to intercede for them.

Children can be used powerfully in prayer. As I was writing this book, I was reminded about an article I wrote in 1983 for a newsletter we used to send out called, *The Children's Banquet.* The title of the article was *Training Children To Intercede.*

Intercession. It's certainly NOT for children, right? After all, children cannot develop in God's "deeper" things.

A twelve-year-old prophesy? No, he must be "in the flesh."

These were a few of my misconceptions when I first started to work in children's ministry. I thank God that I have changed my thinking.

He showed me how to teach children about the gifts of the Spirit, how to be led by the Spirit of God, and intercession. While preparing to teach on intercession one day, I heard these words in my spirit, "People have not taught children how to intercede because they didn't believe that

CHILDREN AND THE HOLY SPIRIT

children could discipline themselves to really intercede."
But I see children who have the time to intercede while
their parents say, "I'm too busy."

I began to see why children were not really developed
in these areas. People didn't believe children could intercede and so did not take the time to teach them.

I saw in my spirit a children's church where children
would flow naturally in all the gifts of the Spirit, intercession, and worship with our God. However, it didn't manifest itself until one Sunday evening.

During worship that night the Lord told me to have
the children intercede for three youngters who were having problems. I obeyed, told the children and we started
to intercede and groan in the Spirit. Praise God! We
prayed and prayed and interceded for over one hour. It
only seemed like 15 minutes. Then, after the burden lifted, a seven-year-old girl prophesied and encouraged the
children to spend time alone with God. Praise the Lord
for what He is doing in children's ministry. [2]

This article was written in 1983 before we were seeing anything happen with kids like we see happening today.

What I saw back then was a look into the future of an army
of children who were interceding for the lost and evangelizing
the lost.

Just this past summer in 1998, I took some of our ministry

CHILDREN AND THE HOLY SPIRIT

team kids to help minister at Pastor Greg's kids camp in Fergus Falls. One of the girls who came with us was Ashley, who was 13 years old. One night during ministry time, Ashley was laying on the floor weeping and in deep travail. My wife, Debra, went over to check on her and heard her praying, "Daddy, come home."

We have known Ashley for many years and knew that her mother and father were divorced many years earlier, and that her mom was recently remarried. Deb thought this was a bit odd that Ashley would be praying, "Daddy, come home." So she asked her, "What are you seeing?"

Ashley told Debbie that she saw a vision of her dad and some other relatives in hell. Debra and some other girls came over to help Ashley pray for her dad. Wow! God can use kids to do some pretty serious praying. The following is an excerpt from Vann Lane's book *Children Of Revival*. This is another example of a child being used in a mighty way to intercede.

As I mentioned earlier, I did not jump into revival. The first person in my family to enter into what God was doing was my eight-year-old daughter, Whitney. In the very early days of revival, Whitney began to intercede and travail in prayer during the altar calls. Her body would violently shake from head to toe. Sometimes she wailed so loudly that you could hear her above Steve Hill. I am ashamed to admit this, but I didn't encourage Whitney; I actually tried to quench what she was doing. I was afraid and I didn't understand what was going on. I tried to make her stop, but the shaking and crying continued.

One night during a revival service, Whitney began to reach down to the ground with both hands and then lift her hands back up over one shoulder. She repeated this action over and over and over, all the while trembling and weeping. Dana looked at her, bewildered. "Dear God! What is happening to my child?" Dana felt the Lord telling her that Whitney was, in a spiritual sense, reaching down and snatching people from hell. We watched with a mixture of awe and amazement.

At the end of the meeting, we asked Whitney what God had been saying to her while she interceded. What did it mean when she kept pulling her hands down low and then back up over her shoulder? Whitney's answer was a confirmation of what the Lord had already spoken to Dana. Our little girl had been snatching people from hell.

In October of 1995, Whitney shared her testimony of this experience during an evening revival service.

"God was telling me to take people off the earth where it was like they were living in hell, and put them into a stage (a place) where they would live like Jesus on the earth. God told me that if I didn't snatch them out of hell from the earth that they would go down to hell when they died. So I obeyed God and I pulled them up. . .

"Brother Dick Rueben prayed for me and all I could hear in my ears was God saying, 'Whitney, when you get older, you're gonna deliver My people' . . .

"As I reached down, I felt pain in my arms like people feel in hell. But as I reached up, I felt like God running through my arms. I felt love and joy and peace. It felt just wonderful because when I put them down I could just feel the pain that people feel when they go to hell. . ."

At this point in her testimony, Whitney bowed over low and began to weep. Pastor John came over to her and said gently, "Whitney, what would you want to say to other children about this revival?"

Crying softly, her voice breaking, Whitney responded, "Listen to God when He talks to you so you can tell people what He's saying to you."

Pastor John went on to quote Joel 2:28 where it says God will pour out His Spirit and our sons and daughters will prophesy; they will speak for Him. [3]

Since then, Whitney has met one of the men she was interceding for that day. He now travels around the world and testifies that it was the prophetic intercession of a little girl that snatched his soul out of a life destined for hell. As he shows the video of Whitney praying, the anointing of God falls on the audience...and many are saved.

1 AFA.netE The Official Home Page of the American E.

2 Mark Harper, *The Children's Banquet Newsletter* (Port Huron, Michigan, Mark Harper Ministries, 1983), p.1.

3 Vann Lane, *Children Of Revival,* (Shippensburg, Pennsylvania, Destiny Image Publishers, Inc., reprint 1998), pp.44,45.

CHAPTER TEN

A Prophetic Word For America

As I was writing this book, I began to research the Bible for stories of children and youth being used by God. (If this is of God, its foundation must be in the Word of God.) I began to study about Josiah, the eight-year-old king. While I was writing, I began to write prophetically. I will share that "word" later in this chapter, but first let's take a look at the "boy king," Josiah.

II CHRONICLES 34:1 (NAS)
Josiah was eight years old when he became king, and he reigned thirty-one years in Jerusalem.

Stop and think about this for a moment. Would you go to a church where the pastor was eight years old? I have to admit that my flesh would have trouble with it. That would be a real humbling experience, but remember the Lord wants us to be humble.

It's amazing, though, that God trusted the leadership of the entire nation (and not just any nation-His people, the nation of Judah) to an eight-year-old.

How did Josiah do? He destroyed all the altars, which were

built to the pagan gods, and the graven images. The Bible says that Josiah *"did that which was right in the sight of the Lord, and walked in the ways of David his Father."*

Josiah did not have an easy job either, because the kings that came before him were ungodly.

One day Hilkiah, the high priest, found the book of Law in the house of God. (It's amazing that God's law had become so forsaken that it had to be found.) Shaphan, the scribe, read the book of the law to King Josiah.

When Josiah heard the words of the law, a spirit of repentance immediately fell upon him.

II CHRONICLES 34:18—28 (NAS)

18 Moreover, Shaphan the scribe told the king saying, "Hilkiah the priest gave me a book." And Shaphan read from it in the presence of the king.

19 And it came about when the king heard the words of the law that he tore his clothes.

20 Then the king commanded Hilkiah, Ahikam, the son of Shaphan, Abdon the son of Micah, Shaphan the scribe, and Asaiah the king's servant, saying,

21 "Go, inquire of the Lord for me and for those who are left in Israel and in Judah, concerning the words of the book which has been found; for great is the wrath of the Lord which is poured out on us because our fathers have not observed the word of the Lord, to do according to all that is written in this book."

22 So Hilkiah . . . went to Huldah the prophetess,...

24 thus saith the Lord, "Behold I am bringing evil on this place, and on its inhabitants, even all the curses written in the book which they have read in the presence of king of Judah.

25 "Because they have forsaken Me and have burned incense to other gods . . . therefore My wrath will be poured out on this place, and it shall not be quenched."'

26 But to the King of Judah . . .

27 "Because your heart was tender, and you humbled yourself before God, when you heard His words against this place . . .and because you humbled yourself before Me, tore your clothes, and wept before Me, I truly have heard you," declares the Lord.

28 "Behold, I will gather you to your fathers and you shall be gathered to your grave in peace, so your eyes shall not see all the evil which I will bring on this place and on its inhabitants."'

With King Josiah, we see that not only can God use children to minister, but He can also use children to lead and influence the world around them.

The bottom line of the word Josiah received was that God's wrath was going to be poured out on Judah, but it would not happen during Josiah's lifetime. God had mercy on Josiah and his entire generation because of his tender heart and leadership.

Notice how Josiah's obedience not only affected him, but he

influenced his entire generation.

It's also interesting to note in the scripture that when there was ungodly leadership, God would often turn to the children. Notice this pattern:

When Saul rebelled, God anointed a teenager named David to be king. When Eli was in sin, God spoke to a child named Samuel. When Judah had several wicked kings who were idol worshipers, God turned to an eight-year-old boy named Josiah to lead the nation.

At the beginning of 1999, our president stated that the state of our union is strong. How can he say that? We may be strong economically, but we are sacrificing our morals, our values, our children, and our future.

Our children, in the past several years, have been murdering one another in our schools. It seems that our culture is obsessed with sex, drugs, violence, and pornography. In fact the Supreme Court just recently struck down a law designed to protect our children from pornography. What is wrong with our nation when we say that the free speech of pornographers is more important than the minds and hearts of our children?

Our nation leads the world in teen pregnancy. Is the nation strong for those babies who grow up without daddies. Something like 25% of the children in our nation grow up without a father at home. Is this nation strong for the father-less? It seems that Americans are saying that as long as we are prospering economically, our nation is strong.

I believe that this is a prophetic word for our nation, America, right now. America is deserving of God's wrath because we are being led by ungodly leaders. But I don't believe we will see God's wrath, because He delights in mercy.

Ninevah was deserving of God's wrath, but God sent Jonah to Ninevah to warn them of His coming wrath because His desire was to pour out mercy. The result was that Ninevah repented of their sins, and God spared the city.

The following is a quote from *The Chosen Fast* by Arthur Wallis, which was first printed in 1968.

> How is it that fasting can help us here? On the negative side, pride and a too-full stomach are old bedfellows. What was the sin of Sodom? Not primarily that gross form of immorality known anciently as sodomy, now called homosexuality. The Bible says, "This was the guilt of your sister Sodom, pride, surfeit of food and prosperous ease." (Ezekial 16:49) When we look at the nations of the West today where this sin of Sodom is rampant, we can discern the same root causes. History cannot help repeating itself. Given the same conditions, the same malaise inevitably falls. [1]

It's not that I think God's wrath is going to be poured out on our nation right now, but what concerns me is when I think about where we will be in the next twenty years.

We are truly entering a time when evil has become good and good has become evil. Where does it end? Where are our nation's leaders leading us? Where will we be twenty years from now?

I believe that the hope for our nation is our children and our youth. We must reach them now while their hearts and minds are tender. It's not good enough just to reach my own children. We must reach the children of the nation.

Right now, there are hot spots of revival around the country, but we have yet to see a national revival that influences our whole country. I believe we will see a national revival that will be led by our children and our youth. They are the key to reaching the lost youth of our nation. Just as in the time of Josiah, when the adult leaders were ungodly, God turned to a child to bring the nation to repentance.

The children of America know that our nation is not strong. They are the ones growing up in homes without fathers. They are the ones who go to school everyday in fear of their lives. They are the ones with no hope for tomorrow.

But there is an answer and there is hope. If we as Christian leaders will lead our children to revival, then they can jump into the river. Our children only need us to believe in them.

Pastors, Leaders, Churches, Parents, wake up! If we just protect our own children from the evil in the world we will lose our nation to an immoral majority. We are called by God to win our children, but we are also called to influence our nation and the world around us. Let's face it, the politicians of our nation have their minds made up—they are not going to change. If we want to change our nation we must reach the hearts of children and youth while they are still tender.

In the book of Esther we read where she was faced with a decision. Mordecai told her, ***"For if you remain completely silent at this time, relief and deliverance will arise for the Jews from another place, but you and your father's house will perish. Yet who knows whether you have come to the kingdom for such a time as this?"*** Esther 4:14 (NJKV). If she did nothing, deliverance would still come, but God put her in a place and time where she could be a godly influence. She could make a difference.

I believe we are here for such a time as this! Now is the time! You can make a difference. You can make a change that will spark revival in your children, in your church and in this nation. That change begins in your heart!

---

1 Arthur Wallis, *God's Chosen Fast*, (Fort Washington, Pennsylvania: Christian Literature Crusade, reprint 1997), pp.44, 45.

Mark Harper
Mark Harper Ministries

Acts 1:8 says that "He will pour out His spirit on all flesh." Mark Harper believes "all flesh" includes every person, young and old.

Since 1978, Mark has served as associate and children's pastor in three churches and senior pastor at one church. Mark is now traveling worldwide, conducting family revival services and conferences for parents and teachers on leading children in revival.

Mark's ministry is unique in that God has anointed him to minister to the whole family. His approach is fresh, humorous and very practical.

The heart of Mark's ministry is to take the current revival to children and youth. All across the world young people are being filled with the Spirit, speaking in other tongues and getting drunk with Holy Ghost laughter. We have seen children weep and intercede at the altar for hours.

Currently, 4,000 churches worldwide use the Super Church Curriculum Series, which was first published by Mark Harper Ministries in 1988.

Additional materials available from Mark Harper Ministries

SUPER *Church*

SuperChurch Curriculum Series

Super Church Curriculum Series is a curriculum dedicated to teaching children, ages 6-12, the Word of God and leading children in revival.

- **SuperChurch Year One**
    Vol. 1 — *Christian Foundations*
    Vol. 2 — *Learning To Pray*
    Vol. 3 — *Divine Healing*
    Vol. 4 — *Gifts Of The Spirit*

- **SuperChurch Year Two**
    Vol. 5 — *Growing Up Spiritually*
    Vol. 6 — *ABC's Of Faith*
    Vol. 7 — *Walking In Love*
    Vol. 8 — *Our Redemption*

$ 119.⁰⁰

- **SuperChurch Year Three**
    Vol. 9 — *Holy Ghost & Fire*
    Vol. 10 — *The Father's Love*
    Vol. 11 — *Praise & Worship*
    Vol. 12 — *Spread The Fire*

KinderChurch Curriculum Series

KinderChurch Curriculum is designed for preschoolers, ages 3-5. KinderChurch teaches basic Bible principals and trains these little ones to worship God.

- **KinderChurch Year One**
    Vol. 1 — *The Ten Commandments*
    Vol. 2 — *The Fruit Of The Spirit*
    Vol. 3 — *The Armor Of God*
    Vol. 4 — *The Life Of Christ*

125/g 3 mos.

- **KinderChurch Year Two**
    Vol. 5 — *Jesus Is My Best Friend* (Salvation)
    Vol. 6 — *Knowing God* (Discipleship)
    Vol. 7 — *It Pays To Obey* (Obedience)
    Vol. 8 — *Loving God* (Worship)

Worship Tapes Available

These powerful praise and worship tapes will lead children in a closer walk with Jesus.

Orange Ya Glad Ya Love Jesus by Jerre Sibinski
Jesus Is My Best Friend by Jerre Sibinski
Be Like Him by Jerre Sibinski
KinderChurch Praise by Jerre Sibinski and Jill Almquist
Songs For Children by Margie and Mickey
That Makes Up Me by Susan Fletcher
Holy Ghost & Fire by Jerre Sibinski
ABC's Of Faith by Jerre Sibinski
Take Time To Worship by Margie & Mickey

Super Church Live! by Mark Harper

These dynamic tapes for children teach the Word of God in a powerful way they will never forget.

The Holy Ghost Will Take The Chicken Out Of You
Jesus Beat Up The Devil
Prayer Power
God's Medicine For Kids
It Pays To Obey
Sword of The Spirit
The Blood Of Jesus

To order any of the teaching materials above or for more information, please contact Mark Harper Ministries at **800-798-4872.**